Virginius Dabney's Virginia

Virginius Dabney's Virginia

Writings about the Old Dominion

With an introduction by Tom Wolfe and photographs by John Theilgard

Algonquin Books of Chapel Hill
1986

Published by
ALGONQUIN BOOKS OF CHAPEL HILL
Post Office Box 2225
Chapel Hill, North Carolina 27515-2225

in association with
TAYLOR PUBLISHING COMPANY
1550 West Mockingbird Lane
Dallas, Texas 75235

© 1986 by Virginius Dabney. All rights reserved.

For permission to reprint articles and portions of books by Virginius Dabney, the author wishes to express his gratitude to the following:

New York Times Magazine, for "Jamestown Before the Mayflower," © 1957 by *The New York Times*; Doubleday and Company, for excerpts from *Virginia: The New Dominion*, © 1971 by Virginius Dabney, *Richmond: The Story of a City*, © 1976 by Virginius Dabney, and *Across the Years*, © 1978 by Virginius Dabney; *American Heritage*, for "Jack Jouett's Ride," © 1961 by *American Heritage*; *Saturday Evening Post*, for "He Made the Court Supreme," © 1955 by the *Saturday Evening Post*; Dodd, Mead and Co., for excerpt from *The Jefferson Scandals: A Rebuttal*, © 1981 by Dodd, Mead and Co.; the University Press of Virginia, for excerpt from *Mr. Jefferson's University: A History*, © 1981 by University Press of Virginia; Algonquin Books of Chapel Hill, for excerpt from *The Last Review*, © 1983 by Virginius Dabney.

The author is grateful to Richmond Newspapers, Inc., for permission to reprint articles that first appeared in the *Richmond Times-Dispatch*.

Printed in the United States of America

LIBRARY OF CONGRESS CATALOGING-IN-PUBLICATION DATA
Dabney, Virginius, 1901–
  Virginius Dabney's Virginia.
  Writings originally published 1925–1984.
  1. Virginia—History. I. Title. II. Title: Virginia.
F226.5.D33   1986   975.5   86-7869
ISBN 0-912697-42-3

This book is affectionately dedicated to James Sidney Watkinson, who moved to Virginia, became highly successful in his chosen field, and having married my daughter became the father of four of my beloved grandchildren.

Contents

List of Illustrations	ix
Introduction by Tom Wolfe	xi
Prefatory Note	xvii
"Poor Old Virginia"	1
Virginia	6
Jamestown Before the Mayflower	20
The Knights of the Golden Horseshoe	29
Beginning of a Revolution	38
Jack Jouett's Ride	47
George Washington's Boozing Gardener	56
He Made the Court Supreme	60
The Jefferson Scandals	74
Life at the Early University	94
Edgar Allan Poe in Richmond	104
The Decline of Virginia	118
General Lee Takes Command	128
Charlottesville in the 1910s	137
A Prophet of the New South	147
A Remedy for Virginia's Business Slump	156
1932: The Confederates Return	161
Richmond Starts Its Third Century	178
Skyway in the Blue Ridge	187
L'Envoi	194

List of Illustrations

Between pages 42 and 43
Powder Magazine, Williamsburg
Jamestown Island
Site of battlefield, Great Bridge
Waterfront at Norfolk
Where *Merrimac* and *Monitor* clashed, Hampton Roads
View of Gwynn's Island, from Mathews County
Mount Vernon, seen from the south
Monument to Mount Vernon slaves

Between pages 122 and 123
Confederate trench, near Richmond
Robert E. Lee Statue, Monument Avenue, Richmond
View from Main Street, Richmond
Ruins of Tredegar Iron Works, Richmond
John Marshall House, Richmond
St. John's Church, Richmond
Virginia State Capitol, Richmond
Shenandoah Valley, from Swift Run Gap

Between pages 186 and 187
Monticello
Vegetable garden at Monticello
Charlottesville, from Monticello
Range, University of Virginia
Cemetery near Port Republic battlefield
Stonewall Jackson Statue, Lexington
Narrow-gauge railroad, Blue Ridge
Looking west from Blue Ridge Parkway

Introduction by Tom Wolfe

I grew up with the impression that the Virginius in the name Virginius Dabney referred to an evolutionary species, after the fashion of the Bufalus Bison, the Anthalopus Bovidae, or the Equus Caballus. I wasn't the only one, either. Dabney was the editor of a newspaper in my hometown, the *Richmond Times-Dispatch*, and when some University of Virginia students published a parody of the *Times-Dispatch* in 1949, they called it the *Virginius Dispatchus*.

They were not happy with the man. Dabney had just written several editorials from which you could conclude that the student body at The University, as it was known, had become a mob of stupefied double-digit-IQ literacy-proof rural gentry. Nobody in Virginia with a high opinion of himself took Dabney's scorn lightly, because in fact he *was* the epitome of the species Virginius. He was one of those newspaper editors who rise up now and again from journalism's trough of mortal error and become the personification of certain values deemed important to the community.

I can't think of a single newspaper editor of that eminence in the United States right now. But remarkably, there were two in Richmond during Dabney's newspaper days. The other was Douglas Southall Freeman, editor of the *Richmond News Leader* and author of one of the great Civil War histories, *Lee's Lieutenants*. Freeman delivered a news broadcast every day at noon over his newspaper's radio station, WRNL, in an accent baked in batter bread. Rain, snow, pestilent humidity, or brain-frying heat notwithstanding, Freeman always began by saying, "Good morning, ladies and gentlemen, it's a beautiful day here on the Riviera of the South." I was twenty-four years old before I realized that this was an example of that common phenomenon of twentieth-century rhetoric, the one-way comparison. Richmond resembled the Riviera, but the Riviera didn't resemble Richmond. Imagine my surprise when I learned that the Riviera was not a city on seven hills, rising up from a muddy river, where respectable men wore white shirts, neckties, and seersucker suits even when it was so hot the doorknobs were mushy. By noon, in Richmond, the seersucker suits all had dark half-moons under the armpits. As a boy I assumed they came that way. I figured they hung on the rack in the men's department of Miller & Rhoads Department Store with the half-moons sewn in.

According to the Douglas Southall Freeman legend, he arose every morning at 2:30, wrote until 4:30, then drove to work, stopping on the way beside a six-story-high statue of Robert E. Lee on his horse, Traveller, in the middle of Monument Avenue. There—or so the legend has it—he got out, snapped his right hand to his forehead in a salute, then got back in his car, and proceeded to the *News Leader* to rally the citizenry around his and the General's high standards.

The Civil War motif was appropriate, for what both Freeman and Virginius Dabney personified was the ideal of the Virginia Gentleman as it existed at the turn of the century. In Virginia the Civil War had a curious and, I would say, salutary effect on the class structure. The war wiped out the assets of practically every prominent family in the state. For the next fifty years, up until the First World War, to be rich was to be déclassé. It meant either you had no roots in the Old Dominion or that your family had not given its all to the Confederate cause. The result was an interlude in which Virginia had what could pass for an aristocracy in the original sense of "rule by the best"—not by the richest but by the best reared, the best educated, the most cultivated, the most devout, the most public-spirited, and, if one need edit, the best connected. It was only an interlude, but it produced many illustrious and altruistic figures such as Freeman and Virginius Dabney. Today, of course, in Richmond, no less than in New York or Dallas or Cincinnati, an aristocrat is anyone with an astonishing amount of money who also made a big contribution to the museum drive last year.

Dabney was born (in 1901) into a set of connections that could scarcely be improved upon in Virginia. His father was a life-long chum and fraternity brother, at The University, of Woodrow Wilson, who became president of the United States when Dabney was fifteen. By blood or long friendships the Dabneys were close to the Jeffersons—which is to say, *the* Jeffersons—*the* Cabells, *the* Davises, *the* Saunderses, *the* Staiges, *the* Bryans, *the* Pinckneys, *the* Tuckers, and on and on. Today no one could remain for long in any such network without being loaded financially. Today merely buying and maintaining the obligatory brace of German or Swedish automobiles is enough to separate the shabby from the genteel.

Dabney's family had very little besides ten acres outside of Charlottesville and his father's pay as The University's sole history professor. Dabney didn't even attend school until he was thirteen. Daddy and Aunt Lucy taught him at home. Finally a small raise in pay made it possible for his father to send him off to Episcopal High School in Alexandria, Virginia, where a year's tuition, room, and board were only $400. He and his father walked the three miles from the railroad station in Alexandria to the school for his enrollment, rather than pay for a taxi. Dabney arrived with his joints aching with frugality. Episcopal High School was one of the two or three most prestigious boarding schools in the South. It was known as The High School. Wags called it T.H.S. instead of E.H.S. After T.H.S., Dabney went to The University. It was The education and The sendoff for an important career in the South, and in that happy interlude it was available to a family that didn't have two cents to rub together, as they said in Albemarle County, home of The University and The Dabneys.

The Dabneys had an ice house and a surrey instead of a refrigerator and an automobile. William McKinley was president, and Queen Victoria had been dead for only seventeen days, when Dabney was born. He saw Halley's Comet the first time it came around in this century, in 1910. He also saw "two world wars, the Korean War, and the war in Vietnam, not to mention the Russian Revolution, the Chinese Revolution, the scientific revolution, and the sexual revolution," as he wrote in 1978 in his memoir, *Across the Years*. In his lifetime "automobiles, airplanes, radio, television, and antibiotics have been invented, abortions have been legalized, and we have put men on the moon, but nobody has come up with a cure for the common cold. Racial segregation has been outlawed."

With the possible exception of antibiotics and William McKinley, Dabney wrote about all of these subjects in the pages of the *Times-Dispatch*. But race was the test for him as it had been for many prominent Southern editors in the nineteenth century. Dabney began urging greater civil rights for black people as early as 1932. In 1943 he called for the desegregation of buses and streetcars in Richmond and for the appointment of black officers to police black neighborhoods. In an era of *de facto* apartheid (throughout the United States) this was a daring proposition. In 1948 Dabney won the Pulitzer Prize for editorial writing.

At the beginning of his newspaper career he was assailed as a liberal or worse. Toward the end he was assailed as a conservative or worse. In fact, he was the enlightened Virginia Gentleman of the finest vintage from start to finish. He had no interest in destroying or even annoying Richmond's genteel establishment. After all, he was part of it. But neither would he let it stand still. He wanted to move it—by leading it in his direction. In that he was probably successful. He takes pride in the fact that Virginia made the transition from apartheid to full political equality and participation without violence and without even any terrible bitterness.

Dabney also did as much as any other single individual to lay to rest the bad feelings between North and South that had persisted since the Civil War. The animosity had been intense at times, particularly in the South, during his youth. He was in his mid-thirties when he cooked up the idea of the Last Reunion. In 1938 it took place: a reunion of 1,800 Civil War veterans, Union and Confederate, at Gettysburg. Most of them were in their nineties. It lasted eight days. In that period the boys swallowed forty-two cases of whiskey. The Blue and the Gray departed with arms around each other's shoulders, baying at the dawn.

Two years ago Dabney published a book about the last Confederate reunion in Richmond, in 1932, which brings me to what fascinates me most about him.

His forty-seven years as a newspaperman constituted merely his first career. When he retired from the *Times-Dispatch* in 1970, he immediately began his second as an author. He had written three books while working for the newspaper: *Liberalism in the South* (1932); *Below the Potomac* (1942), a study of the modern South; and *Dry Messiah* (1949), a biography of Bishop James Cannon, the Prohibition crusader. Since 1970 he has published seven: *Virginia: The New Dominion* (1971), *Richmond: The Story of a City* (1976), *Across the Years* (1978), *Mr. Jefferson's University* (1981), *The Jefferson Scandals* (also 1981), *The Last Review* (1984), and the book now before you. Three of these are voluminous histories: of a state, of a city, and of not a, but The University. Another, *The Jefferson Scandals*, rocked the world of American historiography five years ago by demolishing the popular Brodie thesis: viz., that Thomas Jefferson had sired a backstairs family at Monticello with a slave named Sally Hemings.

Dabney recently completed another book, a history of Virginia Commonwealth University, and is currently at work on still another, an account of certain illustrious dueling nineteenth-century Virginia newspaper editors. He is eighty-five years old and does not slow down, not even on the tennis court, where he was runner-up for the Richmond city championship. In addition to the other connections his family gave him, he seems to be wired with the sturdiest genes imaginable. His father lived to be eighty-seven; and his mother, ninety-eight.

Oh, which reminds me: the name Virginius turns out to be another family legacy. In 1835 Dabney's great-grandfather left Virginia to settle in Mississippi and became so homesick he named his new son Virginius. Virginius I left Mississippi when he grew up and moved to Virginia for a spell and then became a novelist and an editorial writer (for the New York *Commercial Advertiser*). Rather than try to unravel this bit of genetic history, I will leave it to his grandson, Virginius II. He, the noblest of the species, is sure to take care of it in some subsequent tome.

Prefatory Note

From the millions, if not tens of millions, of words that I have written in books, magazines, and newspapers concerning the state of Virginia in its many phases, the editors of Algonquin Books of Chapel Hill have chosen for this volume what they regard as a reasonable sample.

The selections begin with my initial appearance in the *Baltimore Evening Sun* back in 1925 and in H. L. Mencken's *American Mercury* in 1926, on down through nearly sixty years to an extract from my most recent book, *The Last Review*, which was published in 1984.

The reader will doubtless note in the first two selections, produced when I was in my middle twenties, an attempt on my part to write like Mencken. The "Bad Boy of Baltimore" and "Gentleman with the Meat-Axe," who blasted prohibitionists, Ku Kluxers, Comstocks, prehensile politicians, and blue-nosed wowsers, was an idol of many newspapermen in the 1920s and 1930s. A lot of us tried to imitate his muscular style and slashing iconoclasm.

A number of the other pieces presented herewith appeared not long after those referred to, when I was still a young reporter. I cherish the hope that allowance will be made for the author's immaturity.

What I have written concerning Virginia has always been done *con amore*. Even when I have been most critical of the old commonwealth, I have tried to leaven the disparagement with at least a modicum of compensatory praise. At times, I confess, there have been tendencies and actions that strained the bonds of my affection. But there was never a time when I wanted to leave Virginia permanently for any other place on earth. The fleshpots of New York City did not tempt me. That city's febrile pace, cut-throat competition, and lack of good manners combined to cause me to rejoice whenever I left it to return to my native state.

Virginia's greatest men and women, whose names are legion, inspire me. No other American state has produced so many leaders of heroic stature. None can match the eight Virginia-born U.S. presidents.

Admittedly the Old Dominion goes off the rails occasionally. It was untrue to its heritage when its leaders became bemused in the 1950s with the concept of "massive resistance" to the United States Supreme Court's ruling outlawing segregation in the public schools. But as has usually happened before, the leadership came to its senses and put the commonwealth back on the right road.

Virginians are regarded in some quarters as supercilious and as looking down their noses at the so-called lesser breeds. This supposed characteristic is amusingly illustrated in the story of a Virginian who was said to have gone to North Carolina and fallen ill. The doctors there scratched their heads for days in an effort to find out what was the matter. Finally one of them said he thought he had the answer, but he hesitated to give it because the malady, as he saw it, was so rare. Finally he offered to venture his diagnosis: "We have here something that has never been seen before on land or sea, a Virginian with an inferiority complex!"

The jest would have been more opportune a century ago, for Virginians today are much less inclined to snobbishness than their forebears. When members of the Confederate cabinet came to Richmond from all parts of the South soon after the outbreak of the Civil War, some elements of Richmond's high society reacted "much as the Roman patricians felt at the impending arrival of the leading families of the Goths," as Clifford Dowdey put it. Virginia and Richmond are far more cosmopolitan and openminded today than they were when the Union armies were hammering at the gates.

Indeed, both of them have put the Civil War and its lingering trauma behind them, and have enthusiastically entered the modern age. And they have done this without sacrificing their ancient heritage. Many historic shrines have been carefully preserved; the gracious amenities of other days are alive and well; the commonwealth boasts colleges and universities of national stature, as well as widely acclaimed writers and artists.

New hotels and office buildings are rising in Richmond with dizzying speed; in fact, the city almost seems to be exploding. Norfolk, too, is in the throes of a tremendous boom, and its spectacular Waterside development is attracting national attention. The entire Hampton Roads area, with its vast military and naval installations, is one of the greatest such concentrations in the world. High technology is a central factor there, as it is in northern Virginia, with its enormous development of defense industries and similar installations.

Virginia's tourist industry is expanding rapidly. The state and its communities are at last advertising their assets with something like adequacy. It took many years for them to awaken to the fact that their historic shrines, cultural advantages, and scenic attractions are worth billions in annual revenue.

Politics in Virginia is as clean as anywhere in the United States and scandals are virtually unknown. Race relations are also good. Despite the massive resistance aberration, Virginia can at least point pridefully to the fact that in the racial turmoil of the 1950s and 1960s it was the only state on the Atlantic seaboard from Massachusetts to Florida in which the National Guard was not once called out to keep order. And in 1985 the voters of Virginia elected as lieutenant-governor the first black to hold statewide office in the South since Reconstruction.

As for what is usually termed progress, the average Virginian seems to feel that this should not be sought at the expense of characteristics long treasured in the commonwealth—the manners, love of tradition, and leisurely pace so highly valued in other days. What is sought is the golden mean which avoids indiscriminate "boosting," on the one hand, and backward-looking worship of the past on the other . . .

It is my hope that the extracts from my writings published in the pages that follow reflect, in some measure, both the good and the bad in the long history of Virginia. I trust, however, that the good is strongly predominant.

VIRGINIUS DABNEY
Richmond, Virginia

Virginius Dabney's Virginia

"Poor Old Virginia"

(1925)

As set forth in the prefatory note, the two pieces on Virginia that follow, in particular the second, are all-too-obvious reflections of the influence of H. L. Mencken on the style of the young reporter who wrote them.

Virginia, admitted to be one of the notoriously unprogressive states of the Union by everybody except Gov. E. Lee Trinkle, who recently declared in a public address that anyone caught talking about "poor old Virginia" should be "shot at sunrise," is faced with another four years of government by the well-oiled political machine which is responsible for the defeat of almost all the progressive movements launched within the commonwealth for more than a generation.

A new governor will be nominated in the Democratic primary next August, this being, of course, equivalent to election. The campaign for the nomination is getting under way with only two candidates enjoying the least chance of success.

Harry F. Byrd, one of the three men who control the machine, and through it the state government, is one of these candidates, and at the present time appears to have an excellent prospect of securing the nomination. It is, of course, obvious that if he is elevated to the governorship the faithful "organization" men who put him in will have to be given their due share of the spoils. The net result will be that the machine will prey on the vitals of the commonwealth for another gubernatorial administration.

G. Walter Mapp is the other aspirant to the executive chair who is conceded a chance. He has almost as consistent a "machine"

From the *Baltimore Evening Sun*, May 15, 1925.

record as his rival but, being less influential with the leaders of the ring, is not getting the support of the organization to any appreciable extent.

Mr. Mapp is, however, an ardent "dry," and it is believed that the Virginia Anti-Saloon League, headed by the Rev. David Hepburn, well-known Methodist crusader, will support him largely. The Methodists and Baptists form a large portion of the Virginia electorate, and if the Reverend Mr. Hepburn can swing his cohorts into line Mr. Mapp may make more of a dent in the opposition than is anticipated. It is said, too, that the pastors of the state, regardless of denomination, are inclining toward Mr. Mapp at this stage of the race.

Virginians are, therefore, faced with the alternative of casting their ballots for the most active member of the machine in the state, or for a man who has been closely identified with the organization and, just as bad, is a pronounced prohibitionist and author of the Mapp law by which statewide prohibition was introduced in 1916. Truly a discouraging dilemma for the voters of the Old Dominion.

As to the campaign declarations of Messrs. Byrd and Mapp, the latter has thus far shown himself the more progressive of the two. He has come out in favor of some first-rate reform measures, such as equalization of the absurdly unjust system of taxation and abolition of the fee system, which enables many constables, sheriffs, and the like to gather in much larger incomes than the judges of the state supreme court.

With regard to the liquor question, Mr. Mapp solemnly avers that he is for "firm but not fanatical" enforcement of prohibition. This pronouncement is capable of various interpretations. The present state prohibition law, adopted by the legislature at its 1924 session, is regarded by many of the thinking people of the state as outrageously stringent. Whether Mr. Mapp would concur in this judgment is certainly doubtful. He probably does not consider the state dry law too severe, or its strict enforcement as "fanatical."

Mr. Byrd may set forth his position clearly on some of the important issues as the campaign progresses, but to date he has remained judiciously silent on many of them. The present outlook is that he will continue to keep mum on certain questions, such as the fee system, or give out only some innocuous statement, for fear of alienating the notorious courthouse rings and other bulwarks of the organization.

With regard to the dry laws, Mr. Byrd has said nothing to date. He has a record favorable to prohibition on which his supporters are counting to woo some of the Baptists and Methodists from the Mapp standard.

The gubernatorial menu offered the Virginia voters is, therefore, by no means an appetizing one. Neither of the candidates is properly fitted to occupy the executive chair, although in saying so no reflection upon the integrity of either is intended.

Many Virginians were hopeful some months ago that the long-awaited Moses had arisen to lead them out of the wilderness. Congressman R. Walton Moore, one of the few public men in the state possessing real ability, was known to be thinking seriously of shying his hat into the gubernatorial ring, and the news was received by the thinking portion of the population with great jubilation. Mr. Moore, however, must have concluded that this intelligent section of the electorate comprised too small a proportion of the voters, for he decided to stay where he is. It is doubtful if he could have been elected governor. The apathy of the Virginia voting population is such that the machine is almost always able to muster enough strength at the polls to swamp the comparatively small opposition which shows itself.

At the risk of being ordered by Governor Trinkle to face a firing squad at dawn, in accordance with his recent *ex cathedra* pronunciamento that critics of Virginia should be shot at sunrise, we repeat that the state is one of the most backward in the Union. To say that she is the most backward of all would be putting it too strongly. Mississippi seems to be holding on to forty-eighth place in most respects as we gallop to the press, and there are doubtless a few other commonwealths occupying lower rungs on the ladder than the Old Dominion. But Governor Trinkle was simply kidding himself when he told a group of super-heated boosters not long ago that Virginia stands in the front rank among the states. This pronouncement of his was evidently a part of his Babbittic "boost, don't knock" program, which has made him consistently impatient of criticism directed toward the state or its government.

It deserves a place in the oratorical hall of fame along with the same speaker's proud boast when he seconded the nomination of Senator Howard Glass for the presidency at the late Democratic marathon.

"No one can point the finger of scorn at Carter Glass!" thundered the governor of Virginia to the delegates in Madison Square Garden—and he added with even greater emphasis, "except with pride!"

Some competent observer remarked in the public prints next day that most of the speeches at the convention would soon be consigned to the limbo of forgotten things, but that this gem from the tongue of Governor Trinkle unquestionably deserved immortality.

As an inveterate booster Governor Trinkle ranks with the most orthodox Kiwanian. He maintains, for instance, that Virginia's roads are being built with reasonable dispatch, whereas the truth of the matter is that highway construction in the state is far from what it should be.

This is mainly due to the foolish failure of the voters to authorize the issuance of bonds for road building in 1923, the overwhelming defeat of the bond issue in the referendum of that year being largely chargeable to the efforts of the machine in general and to Harry F. Byrd, gubernatorial candidate, in particular. Virginia is stuck in the mud as a result, and will probably remain so for some time.

A bond issue for education is being ardently sought by the heads of the institutions of higher learning in the state, chief among whom is President Edwin A. Alderman of the University of Virginia. Undaunted by the walloping given the bond issue for roads, they are bending every effort toward securing the adoption of this method of financing improvements and enlargements in the educational institutions.

It is a virtual certainty at this time, however, that neither the legislature nor the people can be persuaded that bonds should be issued by the state for any purpose. Meanwhile North Carolina, which a few years ago was far behind Virginia in almost every respect, is forging correspondingly ahead of her, thanks to bond issues for roads and education.

Virginia's woes cannot all be saddled upon the back of the machine. In appraising the causes for the state's backwardness the people of the commonwealth should come in for their share of the blame. It is their indifference to matters of public concern which makes it possible for the machine to maintain its stranglehold. For example, the percentage of eligible Virginia voters who cast their ballots in the recent presidential election was only 17.95, while 48.73 percent of the eligibles in the five states surrounding Virginia voted in November. Maryland, with 390,095 fewer persons eligible, cast 235,453 more votes than the Old Dominion, the percentage of eligibles visiting the polls being 42.02.

In fairness let it also be said that Governor Trinkle's predecessor, Westmoreland Davis, the first anti-machine candidate elected to the governorship in twenty years, was certainly no paragon as an administrator of Virginia's affairs. He would never have secured the nomination had it not been for the fact that the organization's allegiance was divided between his two opponents. Under Davis Virginia prospered no more than she has under Trinkle, but the state was at least given a four-year respite from the control of the ring, something that will not happen again before 1929—if then.

Virginia

(1926)

My reference in this article to Jefferson M. Levy's acquisition of Monticello was altogether unfair. Nothing is said of the debt owed by the nation to Mr. Levy and to his uncle, Commodore Uriah Levy, USN, for saving Jefferson's home from ruin. Partly at my instigation, the grave of Rachel Levy on the grounds was rehabilitated in 1985 by the Thomas Jefferson Memorial Foundation, and a tablet placed there recognizing the invaluable services of the Levys in preserving Monticello.

Mythology

Since that great day three centuries ago when the *Mayflower* landed her cargo of witch-burners on our coasts, the Brahmins of Massachusetts have persisted in proclaiming Plymouth as the nation's birthplace and their state as the fount of American culture and democracy. The First Families of Virginia have just as persistently retorted that Jamestown was settled thirteen years before Plymouth and that it was the Old Dominion and not the Bay State that played the leading part in the upbuilding of early America. Nothing seems to stick quite so firmly in the proud craws of the loyal Virginians of today as these claims of the New Englanders. For while they are themselves by no means guiltless of creating historical myths, they are hardly the equals of the descendants of the sainted Pilgrims. If they are reluctant to admit that Washington's Farewell Address was penned by Alexander Hamilton, or that Jefferson deserves little or no credit for the Louisiana Purchase, or that Monroe's part in the promulgation of the Monroe Doctrine was limited, their output of balderdash can scarcely be compared to that of the estimable sons of the Bay State.

From the *American Mercury*, November 1926.

The favorite legend nurtured by New Englanders is that the beginnings of American constitutional history are to be found in the Mayflower Compact. It seems to matter little to them that Virginians had representative government long before the *Mayflower* sailed, and few of them, even today, can be brought to admit that the year 1607 antedated the year 1620. Unfortunately for the peace of mind of highly patriotic Virginians, the Massachusetts historians have persuaded nearly all the people of the North, East, and West that American institutions had their sole origin in the civilization of the Puritans. Right-minded authors and editors in the Old Dominion are thus kept in constant ferment combating this nefarious propaganda and consigning its sponsors to everlasting damnation.

With the perennial wrangle as to whether the blood of a Brahmin or that of an F.F.V. is of deeper indigo I am not especially concerned. The fact is that the greater part of the aristocracies of both the Bay State and Virginia came to flower on this continent. Each sprang in large measure from the English merchant class. Only a handful of the forebears of the haughty Massachusetts gentry of today could boast on their arrival of a coat-of-arms, while a very small proportion of Virginia's puissant First Families can trace their descent from the Cavaliers.

Surgery

Virginia's present boundaries date from 1863, when West Virginia was admitted to the Union as a separate state. Following King James's Virginia Grant of 1609, describing the commonwealth as extending into the interior "West and Northwest," it modestly claimed the entire territory from which have since been carved the states of Kentucky, Ohio, Indiana, Illinois, Michigan, and Wisconsin. By the Northwest Ordinance of 1787 the region north of the Ohio River and east of the Mississippi was detached from the Old Dominion and organized as the Northwest Territory. Five years later Kentucky was admitted as a separate state. This left Virginia with only its present area and that which subsequently became West Virginia.

The surgical operation performed on it during the Civil War

deserves honorable mention. The Constitution forbade the dismemberment of any state without its consent, but this slight obstacle was easily surmounted. Practically all of the western Virginians who sided with the South were in the Confederate army, so a group of 100 percent Americans in that part of the state proceeded, during the absence of the Confederates, to get themselves "elected" to the "Legislature." This "Legislature" convened at Wheeling and notified the government at Washington that it was the Virginia Assembly. The claim was acknowledged by the Great Emancipator and the radicals in Congress, and the Wheeling patriots decided to create the state of West Virginia. When that great commonwealth was admitted to the Union in 1863 a legislature was duly elected, while the noble body which had engineered the dismemberment proceeded to take up its abode in Alexandria, then held by the Northern army, and again to proclaim itself the legislature of Virginia. Everyone knew the government of Virginia was located at Richmond, but the farce was carried out for the remainder of the war and for some time thereafter, with a "governor" of Virginia sitting at Alexandria. After Appomattox the radicals at Washington treated Virginia as a state insofar as getting its consent to the Thirteenth Amendment was concerned, but as a conquered province when it came to accepting its representatives in Congress. Thus in open defiance of the Constitution came into being the sovereign state of West Virginia, "the bastard offspring of a political rape."

Beating the Tom-Toms

The Virginia of today is quite different from that of 125 years ago. Once the first state of the Union, it is now merely one of the forty-eight. Until 1820 it was the most populous commonwealth in the country. Now it is twentieth. Its influence on the affairs of the nation is slight and it has lost its old prestige. We hear sneering allusions on every hand to poor old Virginia's lamentable flop. Its citizens endured these taunts for years with equanimity. They argued that the commonwealth had been laid waste by the Northern armies and that no one could expect the state to resume her leadership for a long period. Time passed but still Virginia lagged.

Its oft-repeated alibis would no longer hold water, but the innate conservatism of its leaders held them inactive. The cultured, old-fashioned Virginia gentleman scorned the idea of shouting the attractions of his native state from the housetops. The rest of the country would have to discover them for itself. No Virginian of the old school had any intention of making a bounding and bawling mountebank of himself in imitation of the uncouth boosters in the more up-to-date sections of the Republic. He asked only to be left in peace in his romantic Zion with his volume of Thackeray, his mint julep, and his apocryphal memories.

But soon the boosters descended upon the land. "These moss-backed fossils have been running the state long enough," they bellowed. "All they do is talk of Virginia's past. We've got to put some pep into this thing! It's up to us to sell Virginia to the world!" So the Virginia State Chamber of Commerce was founded in 1924. And then came the rest of the live-wire organizations. Governor E. Lee Trinkle, their roaring leader, in his closing message to the General Assembly of 1926, spoke of them in the following high terms:

"A State Chamber of Commerce, hitherto unknown in the Commonwealth, has been organized with efficient, patriotic men at its head, working together with a real fervor for the advancement of the State as a whole. I feel, too, that I can point with pride to the work that is being done by Shenandoah Valley, Inc., Southside, Inc., Southwestern Virginia, Inc., and Rappahannock, Inc., and our various Chambers of Commerce, Rotary, Kiwanis, Lions, and Civitan Clubs, all now surging with an intense interest in the progress of the State."

As a result of this great awakening hundreds of thousands of dollars are being spent in advertising Virginia. It was said a few years ago that Hampton Roads, the greatest landlocked harbor on the continent, had been given the state by God and that Virginians were evidently waiting patiently in the confident expectation that God would also develop it. Not so today. The go-getters are seeing to it that Hampton Roads' light is not concealed behind any species of bushel. Similarly the campaign for the Shenandoah National Park was put over the top with little difficulty. Drowsy sons of the Old Dominion were prodded into action and the needed $1,250,000 was pledged in short order. The cities and towns of the state, with an excess of zeal and a corresponding shortage of modesty, are expressing their civic pride through the medium of automobile tags bearing such slogans as: "Richmond And Proud Of It," "Norfolk Where Prosperity Is A Habit," "Boost Bumpass."

Even Richmond, the ancient capital of the Confederacy, has succumbed. No better illustration of the change that has come over Virginia can be cited than the recent metamorphosis in the Richmond Chamber of Commerce. Early this year a member of the chamber wrote a letter to one of the local papers protesting that the organization was "absolutely dead" and that it was nothing more than a place where "blue-blooded F.F.V.'s often gather to listen to one another's stale talk." Immediately the paper began belaboring the chamber unmercifully, accused it of being almost defunct, and declared that what the city wanted was results. Other dissatisfied idealists chimed in, and it was decided that something must be done. An Inter-Club Council, composed of representatives of all the forward-looking organizations in the city was formed at once as an auxiliary to the chamber. And Richmond was put on the map. When it was host not long ago to a Rotary convention every effort was made to demonstrate to the visiting back-slappers that Richmond appreciated this signal honor. The streets were bedecked with flags, automobiles carried placards bearing the generous invitation, "Rotarian Ride With Me," and the keys of the city were handed over to the high priests of pep. Richmond's red-hot boosters are eagerly anticipating the not distant day when the city can boast a population of 200,000, but they quake with apprehension at the thought that Norfolk may at any moment annex Portsmouth and thus wrest from the capital the proud distinction of being the chief metropolis of the state. In their hearts rankles the crushing realization that Atlanta's population is more than 30,000 greater than Richmond's.

Eddie Guest paid the Confederate capital an official visit early this year. The city of James Branch Cabell was thrown into a furor at the prospect of seeing the Poet of the Plain People in person.

The local newspapers heralded his coming with daily eulogies for two weeks before his arrival. More than 2,000 people, the largest gathering that had attended a similar function in years, paid a dollar each to hear one of Eddie's inspiring lectures at the city auditorium. He was invited to address the legislature. Bookstores took advantage of this unprecedented publicity to put on prominent displays of his works and were rewarded by large sales. Eddie so enraptured the local literati that they were moved to express themselves in verse. One of them gave vent to his enthusiasm in a touching lyric printed in a Richmond paper and entitled, "Eddie Guest, You Come Again!"

Thus it is evident that Virginia has roused itself from its torpor and is following the example of the more "progressive" and forward-looking commonwealths. Having drifted along for years in a semi-comatose state, it is now engaged in selling itself to the world. If the blasts of Virginia's advertisers have thus far created smaller atmospheric disturbances than the siroccos generated by the boosters of Florida and California, the explanation lies in the newness of the Virginia movement. Boosting in the Old Dominion has already taken every form except that manifested on a large electric sign displayed in front of a New York church and bearing the simple words "Boost Jesus." Virginia may even come to that, in time.

F.F.V.'s

What of those old-fashioned Virginia gentlemen who a few years ago were so loath to seek publicity for their native state? Have they joined the Rotary Clubs? Have they become salesmen of Virginia?

It is safe to say that the vast majority of these scions of the pioneers still feel the greatest repugnance for the buffooneries of the go-getters. They are anxious for the Old Dominion to recover her lost prestige, but they are utterly unable to comprehend how that end is to be achieved through perpetual bleating about Service and Vision. To the Virginia aristocrat the methods of the boosters are oafish and barbaric. True, some of them have been dragooned into joining the luncheon clubs. The spectacle of a gray-haired Episcopal rector singing asinine songs, banging his fellow Kiwanians on the back and calling them Bob or Jim when he scarcely knows them by sight, is, indeed, a dolorous one. There are others who feel a genuine interest in the welfare of the state, but have declined to join the clubs under any conditions. And there are still others who much prefer the Virginia of the Old South to the modern article. To this last-named group of ultra-conservatives the doings of the he-men are detestable. They feel that Virginia has already been robbed of much of her pristine charm, and they cling desperately to what is left. For example, they oppose the scheme of a Shenandoah National Park on the ground that it will bring millions of Babbitts into the state and tend to divest it of what little remains of its individuality.

Thus it will be seen that there is a large group of Virginians who refuse to echo the yawps of the go-getters. This group is, indeed, much larger than in the majority of states. It includes, generally speaking, the members of the First Families—those Virginians who for 300 years and more have contributed the largest share to the upbuilding of the commonwealth. They are offering stout resistance to the wave of Babbittry which has engulfed the country. If their opposition has not always been evident to the casual visitor, it is nevertheless real. That opposition, in accordance with traditional Virginian etiquette, is generally expressed *sotto voce*, and thus cannot be heard above the *fortissimo* whooping of the boomers. The Service Clubs get most of the publicity and make all the noise, but it does not follow that Virginia has completely capitulated to them. On the contrary, there are few, if any, states in which the Kiwanian lump is leavened with so stiff an ingredient of sense.

Rotarianism finds its toughest sledding in the Tidewater and Piedmont sections. Within this region are situated the oldest cities and towns—Richmond, Petersburg, Norfolk, Williamsburg, Fredericksburg, Alexandria, and Charlottesville. To the people there the current frenzy for larger and larger cities, with taller and taller skyscrapers and bigger and better smokestacks, is altogether incomprehensible. As I have said, it is the civilized element which serves as a partial check to the schemes of Mr. Babbitt. For example, it was recently suggested that the old courthouse at Charlottesville, in which Jefferson frequently attended court, be torn down and a modern structure be erected in its place. At about the same time the Richmond boomers were moved to bring forward a plan for razing the home of John Marshall in order to extend the playground of a public school. Both suggestions were scotched after a hard struggle by citizens who have been able to retain their reverence for tradition and their appreciation of historical associations. Another uplifting scheme was partially carried out before the people of sense were aware of what was up. Several of the old brick walks in historic Capitol Square at Richmond were torn up and replaced with concrete. Asked to explain this vandalism, the superintendent of buildings and grounds explained that "brick walks were all right years ago but they are out of date now." "We want to make the square modern," this talented landscape gardener declared. Immediately upon the publication of this highly illuminating pronunciamento a tremendous howl went up and the superintendent suddenly concluded to leave the remaining brick walks unmolested.

Relics of the Past

In the Virginia of the eighteenth century there was as great a social distance between the opulent planters on the one hand and the masses of the people on the other as that which separated the nobles from the yeomanry in Europe. Although the Virginia of today is almost 75 percent rural, the landed proprietor with his thousands of acres and hundreds of slaves has, of course, vanished long ago. The last vestiges of this feudalistic system were obliterated by the Civil War. Social distinctions in present-day Virginia are based more largely upon wealth than upon birth. While members of the old families often point with satisfaction to their family trees, there are no social barriers separating them from the bourgeoisie. It has been aptly said that in twentieth-century Virginia "bank notes are more than coronets and simple flasks than Norman blood." If there is in the state a single club, circle, or other similar organization into which anyone with a few thousand in the bank and a fair knowledge of the amenities will not be readily admitted, I am not aware of its existence. And if to these attributes be added a well-stocked cellar, the combination is irresistible. Indeed, where membership in social clubs is concerned, the possessor of a corpulent bankroll who is of dubious progeniture is frequently regarded as preferable to one rejoicing in the most patrician lineage but lacking the roll, for dues are sometimes heavy.

If the landed aristocracy of the Old Dominion is a thing of the past, there remain many of the beautiful old Colonial mansions builded long ago by members of that aristocracy in Tidewater, Piedmont, and Valley Virginia. The most famous are Mount Vernon, Arlington, and Monticello. The last-named has recently become a national shrine, having been purchased from the Hon. Jefferson M. Levy, who had almost succeeded in ruining it by installing canopied beds surmounted by the imperial L, granite lions, heavy gilt furniture, and similar monstrosities. Many of these stately mansions standing amid groves of ancient oaks have been preserved in all their original charm, but hardly a dozen in all Virginia remain in the hands of the families which erected them. In some cases those families have died out or moved away, while in others poverty has made necessary the sale of the ancestral home. The consequence is that a large proportion of the Colonial estates are now in the hands of wealthy outsiders. Unfortunately, some of them have been purchased by loutish Middle-Western captains of industry or Northern *nouveaux riches* whose idea of the proper way to furnish an old Virginia home is to throw away the mahogany and secure overstuffed lounges from Saginaw, Mich.

Moronia

Virginia, like the other states of the Republic, has its uplifters bent on legislating morality into the populace. Except in the case of Prohibition, however, the wowsers have had hard going. It was in 1914 that the wets were routed. In that fatal year of grace was passed the Enabling Act, by which the legislature authorized a statewide referendum on Prohibition. With the passage of this act the forces of righteousness launched an intensive campaign against the powers of darkness. Renowned exhorters were imported and the electorate was besought to banish the unholy liquor traffic. Hundreds of church meetings were held. When the day of the referendum arrived, bells were tolled, hymns were caroled, the Scriptures were read, and prayers were offered throughout the state. Such a high pitch of emotional fervor was thus worked up among the Christians by the evangelical sorcerers that they actually were persuaded for the moment that a vote to retain local option was equivalent to a vote for Belial. The result was that the wets went under by a majority of almost two to one. In 1916 the legislature passed a state Prohibition law and Virginia has since been officially dry. Actually things are, of course, different. Virginia is one of the leading states in the number of stills seized within its borders since Volstead was sainted. While there is little prospect at this time of putting through the pious General Assembly any drastic modifications of the state dry law, several of the legislators have, of late, dared to question whether Prohibition rests on a plane of complete equality with revealed religion. One of the assemblymen, for example, recently denounced the superintendent of the Virginia Anti-Saloon League in fierce terms, while another sharply denounced both the superintendent and Prohibition. The latter also charged that "Richmond newspaper editors write dry editorials but fail to decline a good drink of liquor." The fanatics are thus far from being in complete control.

The legislative session of 1926 was also remarkable for the squelching of two bills making the teaching of the federal Constitution and the reading of the Bible compulsory in public schools. Both of these measures were slain in committee. A Methodist clergyman in the Assembly announced his intention of sponsoring a bill outlawing the hideous and nefarious doctrine of evolution. He never introduced it, for he soon found on investigation that it was certain to be defeated. The Baptists of the state, who, with the exception of the Methodists, have the largest membership of any Virginia denomination, were the leaders in the fight against the Bible Bill. They unanimously passed resolutions at their annual convention condemning the bill as "an invasion of the rights of conscience and a violation of religious liberty," and later presented an able memorial to the legislature which might be perused with profit by Kluxers and other such apostles of tolerance. The principal advocates of the Bible Bill were the Methodists and the self-styled Patriotic Welfare Committee, which last was also behind the Constitution and Anti-Evolution Bills. This body of 100 percent Americans is composed of representatives of the Ku Klux Klan, Daughters of America, Patriotic Order of Sons of America, Junior Order of United American Mechanics, Order of Fraternal Americans, and Sons and Daughters of Liberty. It has failed in everything it has undertaken. It first came into prominence during the summer of 1925, when it made a ludicrous attempt to prevent the erection at Richmond of a statue of Columbus, on the ground that he was a Catholic and a "furriner." The opening paragraph of the committee's statement of its alleged reasons for opposing the statue contained these chaste and grammatical lines:

"Believing the citizens are anxious to know why citizens objected to the raising of a monument to one Christopher Columbus, we submit this article, in the beginning we desire to say not through any religious prejudice has there been objection raised but purely upon historical lines, inasmuch as our histories deny the fact that the said Christopher Columbus was the discoverer of America therefore patriotic men and women who believe in dealing justice where same is due, believe that the real discoverer should be recognized if such monuments are to be erected. . . . As we surely favor the erection of a monument anywhere, any time, to any of our noble patriotic American heroes, New York may boast of a Columbus Square and Washington of its monument, yet Virginia, the Mother State of the South, should ever erect monuments to the patriots that are dear to all Americans."

In addition to refusing to pass the measures advocated by the dolichocephalics, the Assembly of 1926 gave its approval to several highly beneficial bills sponsored by Governor Harry F. Byrd who, fortunately for the state, is not a member of the "boost, don't knock" school. When he took office he saw the woeful inefficiency of the state government, and courageously set out to remedy this condition. His programme is generally regarded as the most salutary inaugurated by any chief executive of Virginia in at least a generation.

Teaching the Young Ideas

The institutions of higher education in Virginia are laboring under the serious disadvantage of receiving practically no support from the state. Out of every dollar raised by taxation only 6.2 cents go to higher education, this being the lowest allotment in the Union save in backward Georgia. The consequence is that state-supported institutions of collegiate rank are unable to do much in the way of research. A more cheering aspect of the educational situation is the entire absence of that relic of barbarism, the heresy hunt. With teachers in North Carolina continually belabored by earnest pastors who adhere to the doctrines of Bryanism, and with Tennessee and Mississippi already committed to the literal interpretation of Genesis, educators in Virginia are free to embrace Darwinism, and they do not hesitate to do so, even in the sectarian institutions. Anyone who attempts to hamper scientific research by an appeal to Scripture receives only loud guffaws and is speedily laughed out of court.

The University of Virginia is commonly regarded by the more righteous citizens of the commonwealth as a sinkhole of iniquity, but not because the members of the faculty acknowledge their arboreal ancestry. The youth who matriculates there is not eternally coddled and pestered by professors, nor is he spied on by hired snoopers, as is the case in many other universities. This, of course, is not at all to the taste of the Pecksniffs of the state, who hold to the conviction that the student body is made up of pampered Sybarites spending their time in bacchanalian orgies. This naive estimate of the university cannot be justified. The per capita consumption of booze by the undergraduates is no greater than in Wake Forest College.

Aside from this, the university is one of the most beautiful in America or Europe. Its grounds and buildings were designed by Thomas Jefferson and were laid out under his personal supervision. Visitors from all parts of the world are struck by the Hellenic loveliness of its architecture, the stately beauty of its arcades and serpentine walls, mellowed by the passage of years. On the grounds and in the adjoining town of Charlottesville is probably as much first-rate statuary as can be found in any place of equal size on the planet. William and Mary College, located in the historic town of Williamsburg, was founded in 1693, and is the oldest college or university in the country with the exception of Harvard. It numbers among its alumni Thomas Jefferson, John Marshall, James Monroe, John Tyler, Spencer Roane, Benjamin Harrison, Littleton Waller Tazewell, and many other august celebrities. Then there is Randolph-Macon College, at Ashland, named for John Randolph of Roanoke and Nathaniel Macon of North Carolina. When Randolph was asked by the college authorities if he would permit this institution for the education of young Methodists to be named after him, that ingratiating statesman replied: "Yes, you may use my name, for when educated they will cease to be Methodists."

Today and Tomorrow

While it is obvious that Virginia occupies no such place today as it held at the opening of the last century, its current contributions to civilization are perhaps not quite as infinitesimal as might be supposed. It is moderately well represented in the fine arts, and an examination of *Who's Who* reveals that the number of Virginians in it is almost twice as great as that for any other Southern state and ninth for the entire country.

True, practically all its politicians have capitulated long since to the Anti-Saloon League and may be found doing the goose step behind the Hon. Wayne B. Wheeler. The commonwealth must therefore look to her neighbor, Maryland, for stalwart leadership in combating the tyranny of the dry laws. Finding small comfort in their native habitat, the embattled wets in the Old Dominion rally beneath the standards of those unterrified apostles of individual liberty in the Free State, Governor Albert C. Ritchie and Senator William Cabell Bruce, both of whom are native Virginians.

The question which gives most concern to the illuminati in Virginia today, however, is not quite so much its present as its future status. Only the most fanatic Rotarian will deny that the commonwealth's present position is immeasurably below that of 100 years ago, although it has thus far been able to retain a small share of its former charm and to bring forth a limited number of civilized sons and daughters. But the boom now on threatens to despoil the ancient state of what remains of the glamour that was peculiarly its own. What will Virginia be like in fifty or even ten years? The answer rests with the boosters.

(My apologies for the foregoing smart-alecky slurs on Rotarians, Kiwanians, and members of other service clubs. These juvenile effusions of sixty years ago, aping the words and attitudes of H. L. Mencken, whom I admire in many respects, are without any sort of justification.)

Jamestown Before the Mayflower
(1957)

The impending visit of Queen Elizabeth II to Jamestown [October 1957] will focus world-wide attention on the 350th anniversary festival now in progress there in celebration of the first permanent English settlement in this hemisphere. Commemoration of the settlement—which dates from 1607, thirteen years before the Pilgrim Fathers landed at Plymouth—has been thrown almost into eclipse by the fantastic ballyhoo over the recent voyage of the reconstructed *Mayflower* and that vessel's subsequent commercial exploitation.

The place occupied by the earlier *Mayflower* in the hearts and minds of the American people is secure, but many modern historians feel that the contribution of this ship and its human cargo to the national heritage was well below that of the Jamestown settlers. Nor did the coming of the *Mayflower* have so great an impact on the life of the nation as did the arrival ten years later, in 1630 at Massachusetts Bay (Boston), of the *Arbella*, bearing the first contingent of Puritans. Their more populous settlements soon far overshadowed the small Pilgrim colony at Plymouth.

The way had been paved for these colonizing ventures in Virginia and New England by the destruction of Spanish seapower when England smashed the Spanish Armada in 1588. On the death of Queen Elizabeth in 1603 her successor, King James I, continued the colonizing efforts begun unsuccessfully during her reign. The Virginia Company of London accordingly was formed in 1606.

The *Susan Constant*, the *Godspeed*, and the *Discovery* landed at

From the *New York Times Magazine*, September 29, 1957.

Jamestown the following year and the colony was established there after frightful hardships. Famine, disease, cold, and Indians took a dreadful toll, but when the Pilgrims finally sailed in the *Mayflower* in 1620, Jamestown had a number of epoch-making accomplishments to its credit.

Before embarking for the wilderness beyond the seas, the Pilgrims had spent twelve years in Holland. They were driven there by religious persecution, for they were Separatists who did not like the rites and practices of the Church of England. Wishing to extend their religious principles, to earn an easier livelihood for themselves and their children and to establish themselves under the English flag, they decided to emigrate.

Arriving off the desolate New England coast in late November, the courageous little band suffered intensely. The death toll for the first icy winter was as heavy as it had been for the first disease-infested summer at Jamestown. At each settlement, slightly more than 100 persons had disembarked, and in each at least half died within a few months. But the survivors in both colonies hung on grimly.

Jamestown had been established for more than two decades and Plymouth for one when the Puritan migration began arriving in Massachusetts Bay. The Puritans, like the Pilgrims, were out of favor with the British monarchy and the established church, and were sternly Calvinistic in their beliefs and behavior. Unlike the Pilgrims, they came to these shores direct from England, instead of spending years on the European continent. These Puritans left England well before their increasingly militant compatriots in the mother country succeeded, under the leadership of Oliver Cromwell, in launching a bitter civil war.

So much for the three principal early settlements made by the English on these shores. What did each contribute to our national heritage?

There has been a great deal of misunderstanding concerning this matter, especially in the propagation of the *Mayflower* legend. New England–born historians and orators in the eighteenth and nineteenth centuries succeeded in convincing most Americans that everything in this country began with the *Mayflower*, and that the only other accomplishments of the early colonists were those of the Massachusetts Bay Puritans. Jamestown was either ignored or belittled beyond recognition. The facts are that, in New England, Plymouth was less important than Massachusetts Bay and that the two together were no more important than Virginia.

Consider the statement of Thomas Hutchinson, last royal governor of Massachusetts, in his *History of Massachusetts Bay*, which appeared shortly before the American Revolution. Speaking of the Pilgrim settlement, he wrote that "Virginia [in 1620] was in a dying state, and seemed to revive and flourish from the example of New England." Although Hutchinson's assertion had no factual basis, since Virginia was well established by 1620, it was quoted approvingly by Edward Everett, onetime president of Harvard and successor to Daniel Webster as secretary of state, in his oration of 1824 on the anniversary of the *Mayflower*'s landing.

In 1830, at the bicentennial celebration of Massachusetts Bay, Everett was back in action again. He actually declared that prior to 1630 "various attempts had been made at colonization, at first with very doubtful success, by the Virginia Company"! He also said that in 1630 "there was a feeble colony in Virginia." Near the close of this deliverance, Everett proclaimed that the "venerable foundations of our republic were laid on the *very spot* where we stand by the fathers of Massachusetts."

Everett obviously did not regard the Pilgrims or their Mayflower Compact as of earth-shaking moment, since he credited the Puritans, who came ten years later, with founding the nation. His appraisal of the events is, in general, not too important, but nearly a century afterward his downgrading of the Pilgrim Fathers was to find a supporter in Charles M. Andrews of Yale, one of the great historians of his generation and winner of the Pulitzer Prize for his writings on the colonial period. Dr. Andrews, himself a *Mayflower* descendant, wrote in his book, *The Fathers of New England*, concerning the Pilgrims:

"Their intellectual and material poverty, lack of business enterprise, unfavorable situation and defenseless position in the eyes of the law rendered them almost a negative factor in the later life of New England. No great movement can be traced to their initiation, no great leader to birth within their borders, and no great work of art, literature or scholarship to those who belonged to this unpretending company. The Pilgrim Fathers stand rather as an emblem of virtue than as a molding force in the life of the nation."

Plymouth, as Andrews said, "was vastly overshadowed by her vigorous neighbors," notably aggressive and fast-growing Massachusetts Bay. What were that colony's major achievements?

One of them was its relentless denial of democracy to everyone within its borders, and another was its success in crushing religious freedom. John Winthrop, first governor of Massachusetts Bay, spoke for the rest of the Puritan leaders when he pronounced democracy "amongst civil nations . . . the meanest and worst of all forms of government."

Such was the principle on which the Puritans founded Boston. There was nothing democratic about the government of this colony of "saynts" and "unspottyed Lambs of the Lord," as they termed themselves.

Roger Williams, greatest of all the early New Englanders, was banished by the oligarchy to the snow-covered wilderness in what is now Rhode Island because he believed deeply in democracy and religious freedom. In Rhode Island he did much to build the foundations on which the United States of America was later established, but he did it over the bitter opposition of the Puritans.

The latter were conscientious and sincere when they exiled Williams, Anne Hutchinson, and many others because these men and women refused to obey theocratic edicts. The Puritans were equally sincere when they tortured and hanged Quakers for their beliefs and put to death harmless old women as "witches."

Another statement of Charles M. Andrews—this time to the Colonial Society of Massachusetts in 1932—is pertinent. That internationally known historian said:

"It has been customary . . . to extol the political and social principles of both Pilgrims and Puritans as of great significance, in that they anticipated the doctrines which were destined . . . to become the warp and woof of our American system of government. I doubt this. . . . Nowhere in their writings or applications of policy can we find any generalizations foreshadowing the ideals of the later American republic. . . . None of them would have subscribed to our American doctrines regarding church and state, popular government, or religious freedom."

But the influence of the Puritans was by no means wholly negative. Let us freely acknowledge the nation's debt to them in several important spheres.

First, in education. There was a higher percentage of university graduates among them than any other colony, and they lost little time in setting up a system of public schools. Early Virginia did not manifest a comparable concern for public education. It was overwhelmingly rural, and the vast majority of its people were scattered on small farms or large plantations. Hence public schools were less feasible there than in Massachusetts, with its many small towns. And, in giving us Harvard, by more than half a century the earliest center of higher learning in English America, the Puritans took a pioneering step.

Then there was New England's development of the town meeting, which occurred by a curiously inverted process, described by Samuel Eliot Morison and Henry Steele Commager in their *Growth of the American Republic*, as follows:

"By a town meeting, in which everyone took part, each town settled local affairs such as support of the school, laying out highways, regulations for cutting timber, and deciding when cattle could be turned into meadows and cornfields. Here democracy seeped into New England, unwanted and unsuspected by the founding fathers."

Finally, among the major contributions of the men and women who founded Massachusetts Bay should be mentioned "the Puritan conscience." As with their zeal for education and the establishment of the town meeting, the Puritans influenced this country deeply in the example they set of fortitude, courage, and granite-like devotion to duty.

The "Puritan conscience" must be judged, of course, in the context of the times. In prohibiting the building of beautiful churches and the use of organs and other musical instruments at the services, banning dancing and the maypole, ordering that silk not be worn in any circumstances and even looking sternly upon the wearing of wigs, the early Puritans were reflecting many of the weird preferences and prejudices of their Cromwellian counterparts in England. To them, more than to any other group of "founding fathers" we owe the tendencies in this country during the nineteenth and twentieth centuries toward the adoption of such legislative excrescences as prohibition, anti-evolution laws, and laws banning fishing on Sunday.

Not that the dominies of Plymouth and Massachusetts Bay were averse to inhausting a beaker of beer or rum. There was beer aboard the *Mayflower*, and New England became the chief American seat of rum distilling. The early New Englanders' fondness for rum manufacture was, of course, a vital element in the huge trade in African slaves which centered in Massachusetts and Rhode Island. Slavery was legalized in Massachusetts earlier than in any other colony (1641), and rum was the chief article of barter in exchange for the unfortunates who were rounded up in Africa by New England slave traders.

Leading Massachusetts and Rhode Island families, including the Cabots, the Crowninshields, and the Ellerys, were active dealers in slaves. Boston's Faneuil Hall, sometimes termed "the cradle of liberty," was built with money given by Andrew Faneuil, whose huge profits in the slave trade made this philanthropy possible. The Browns of Providence endowed Brown University with the profits of the traffic.

Despite such indisputable facts as these, a legend has grown up that this country's free institutions all originated in New England, and that democracy and religious liberty put down their first American roots in its rocky soil. Although the early New England chroniclers and orators did much to perpetuate these myths, such modern New England–born historians as Channing, Andrews, and Morison have helped to put the region and its achievements in perspective.

Virginia's contributions should also be kept in perspective. The absurd idea that Jamestown was settled and inhabited by rollicking Cavaliers, and that its atmosphere was one of jollity and mirth, in complete contrast to the dour psalm-singing of the Puritan bluenoses, should be dispelled. Genuine Cavaliers were few and far between in Virginia, a great deal of emphasis was put on religion and religious services there, and the death penalty was prescribed not only for numerous civil offenses but for "impious and malicious speaking against the Blessed Trinity or any person of the Godhead or against the 'knowne' articles of the Christian faith."

Even the doughty Captain John Smith, President of the Council, forbade swearing. Whenever any colonist blistered his fingers at manual labor and let go with loud imprecations, Smith "devised how to have a cann of water powred down his sleeve, with which every offender was so washed (himselfe and all) that a man should scarce hear an oath in a weeke."

Life at Jamestown for the first decade was a desperate struggle for survival. The colonists failed, at times, to plant adequate crops and then wondered why they died of famine. They let their fish-nets "rot and spoile," and then found it strange that fishing was difficult. Many of them, especially the "gentlemen," were averse to manual labor.

Accustomed at home to drinking beer and ale, they were shocked to find that only water was available at Jamestown—water, moreover, that was badly contaminated. No wonder the Spanish ambassador in London remarked that the sparse diet in Virginia was "contrary to the nature of the English" who were known throughout Europe for their "large tabling and belly cheer."

The colonists had gone to Jamestown under a number of grievous misapprehensions. While it would be inaccurate to say that they established the Virginia colony with no other thought in mind than material gain—since they also desired to establish a permanent foothold for British civilization beyond the oceans, to find a route to the South Seas, and to Christianize the Indians—they and their sponsors, the London Company, hoped strongly for monetary rewards. They had been misled as to the possibilities by such fantasies as the play *Eastward Ho!*, presented in London in 1605, which declared that in Virginia "golde was more plentiful than copper is with us . . . all their dripping pans and chamber pots are pure golde." After the settlement of Jamestown was established, in the face of ghastly obstacles, ridiculously optimistic and untrue reports were sent back to England, some by gentlemen of the cloth.

But despite its obvious shortcomings, Jamestown was of enormous importance. Its first charter, granted in 1606 by the Virginia Company, asserted that the inhabitants of the colony "shall have and enjoy all the liberties, franchises and immunities . . . to all intents and purposes, as if they had been abiding and born within this realm of England." This declaration that the English common law would be in full force in the colony was formally reaffirmed in Virginia's "Great Charter" of 1618.

Yet Chief Justice Earl Warren, addressing the American Bar Association in London this summer, made the remarkable statement that "not the least precious part of the cargo brought by the Pilgrims . . . was the common law." The Chief Justice added that they "brought it, not in books, but in their minds." Since the Jamestown settlers had brought it thirteen years before in a written charter, it is a bit difficult to understand why importance is attached to the Pilgrims' admittedly vague version of the common law. This and other statements of Chief Justice Warren in his London address show a belief on his part that the important legacies of English civilization were bequeathed to our forefathers by those who came over on the *Mayflower*. The facts are that, from its inception in 1607, the Virginia colony preserved the institution of trial by jury, except for the five years, 1611–16, when martial law was in force. It granted religious freedom to members of all faiths who would take the oath of allegiance to the British crown. In 1619, the year before the *Mayflower* sailed, the first legislative assembly in the New World met in the church at Jamestown. We have here the beginnings of representative government on the North American continent.

The late Lord Bryce, eminent British historian, termed the Jamestown settlement "one of the great events in the history of the world." Thomas J. Wertenbaker, renowned in both America and Europe as an authority on the colonial period, declared that the Great Charter, conferring upon Virginia the right to representative government, was "the very cornerstone of liberty in the colony and in all America," and added, "it is almost certain that if there had been no Jamestown, there would have been no Plymouth."

Louis B. Wright, recognized for his scholarly writings on our Colonial heritage, says of Jamestown that "no other spot in either hemisphere carries so much significance." He states that if the colony there "had failed, Spain and France ultimately might have divided up all North America between them and the United States of America might never have come into being."

The river still flows past Jamestown, with its ruined church-tower, brooding over the dust of those who died there that a nation might be born. Not only Colonial America but Canada, Australia, New Zealand, and South Africa trace their origins back to this, the first of all Britain's colonies. For here, on the soil of Virginia, in blood, suffering, and death was carried to fruition one of the world's great experiments in self-government and representative democracy.

The Knights of the Golden Horseshoe

(1929)

Since these two articles on the Knights of the Golden Horseshoe were published in 1929, the theory has been advanced that Governor Spotswood and his entourage did not cross the Blue Ridge Mountains at Swift Run Gap and strike the Shenandoah River near the site of today's Elkton, but instead went past Big Meadows through Milam Gap, and reached the stream some fourteen miles below Elkton near the present village of Alma. Be that as it may, the diary of John Fontaine enables us to harbor no doubts as to the basic facts surrounding the expedition, including the vast quantities of alcoholic potations consumed by the rollicking adventurers.

Thursday of this week will mark the 213th anniversary of the arrival of Governor Alexander Spotswood and his "Knights of the Golden Horseshoe" at the top of the Blue Ridge Mountains, whence they saw the Shenandoah Valley spread out below them. For it was on September 5, 1716, after an arduous journey of two weeks through the Virginia wilderness, that this gallant band of adventurers reached Swift Run Gap, on the present highway from Stanardsville to Harrisonburg, and on what is now the Greene-Rockingham county line, and looked down upon that verdant and fertile valley which the Indians called the "Daughter of the Stars." They were almost certainly the first white men who had ever gazed upon the scene.

It was a rollicking and bibulous company of some fifty persons that had set out on the previous August 17 from Germanna, on the Rapidan River in Orange County, for the purpose of explor-

From the *Richmond Times-Dispatch*, September 1 and 22, 1929.

ing the "back country." The town of Germanna, the first German settlement in America, and a place of consequence two centuries ago, was situated in the northeastern corner of what is now Orange County, but it has completely disappeared today. Only the ford in the Rapidan at that point remains.

Alexander Spotswood, who headed the expedition from Germanna, was a man of distinguished ancestry and unusual talents, who had fought under Marlborough at Blenheim and been dangerously wounded. His ancestors included, among others, John Spotswood, Primate of Scotland and Archbishop of St. Andrew's. An ancient chronicler records that the Archbishop was quite proficient at "ye ancient game of golf," and that he could even "lay a stymie in a struggling brother's way." Unfortunately he was charged with lying, gambling, drinking, adultery, incest, and sacrilege, and was deposed as archbishop. In spite of all this, he finished strong, and was buried in Westminster Abbey.

When the "Knights of the Golden Horseshoe" set out from Germanna, the following "gentleman adventurers" were in the party, in addition to the governor: John Fontaine, Robert Beverley, William Robertson, Dr. Robinson, James Taylor, Robert Brooke, George Mason, Captain Smith, Jeremiah Clouder, and a man named Todd whose first name is unknown.

The necessary weapons for protection from Indians and wild beasts were carried, together with a stupendous supply of wines and liquors. In fact, so stupendous was this supply that the forty varlets who accompanied the "gentlemen adventurers" must have devoted a large share of their time to lugging jugs and bottles through the wilds. John Fontaine, whose journal of the expedition is one of the principal sources of information concerning it, sets down that even after they had been on the road for more than a fortnight they still had several sorts of liquors, viz.: "Virginia red wine and white wine, Irish usquebaugh, brandy, shrub, two sorts of rum, champagne, canary, cherry, punch, water, cider, etc." Why "water" should be included in this list is a mystery. The knights do not seem to have made any use of it, except possibly in their ablutions.

The expedition traveled westward, apparently passing through parts of what are now Orange, Madison, and Greene counties, past Mine Run, Mountain Run, and the confluence of the Rapidan and Robertson rivers, and not many miles from President Hoover's present summer camp on the upper Rapidan, to Swift Run Gap, and on to Elkton on the Shenandoah River, a distance of approximately sixty miles over the roads of today.

As the explorers neared the mountains, the country became more and more wild, and they encountered and killed numerous bears and deer. When the foothills of the Blue Ridge were reached, they began meeting rattlesnakes on every hand. Several rattlers were killed daily, and one of the horses was bitten. Other varieties of snakes were also met, one of whom is described by Fontaine as "prodigious." In fact, so numerous are his references to snakes and drinks, that one is tempted to ask if he didn't see some purple elephants, too.

The convivial Fontaine describes the events of September 5, 1716, the day the top of the mountains was reached, as follows:

"We were obliged to have axemen clear the way in some places. We followed the windings of James River, observing that it came from the very top of the mountains. We killed two rattlesnakes during our ascent. In some places it was very steep, in others it was so that we could ride up. About one of the clock we got to the top of the mountain; about four miles and a half, and we came to the very head spring of James River, where it runs no bigger than a man's arm, from under a large stone.

"We drank King George's health and all of the Royal Family's health at the very top of the Appalachian Mountains. About a musket shot from the spring there is another, which rises and runs down on the other side; it goes westward, and we thought we could go down that way, but we met with such prodigious precipices that we were obliged to return to the top again. We found some trees which had been formerly marked, I suppose, by the Northern Indians, and following these trees, we found a good, safe descent. Several of the company were for returning; but the Governor persuaded them to continue about seven miles further, until we came to a large river, by the side of which we encamped."

The "head spring" referred to above is the source of Swift

River, the eastern head spring of the James, and the other spring, a musket shot away, is that of Elk Run, which flows into the Shenandoah at a point about three-fourths of a mile above Elkton, the spot at which the party encamped.

The events of September 7 on the banks of the Shenandoah are interestingly described by Fontaine as follows:

"We crossed the river, which we called the Euphrates. It is very deep. . . . We drank some healths on the other side, and returned; after which I went swimming in it. . . . I got some grasshoppers and fished; and another and I, we catched a dish of fish, and a fish they call chub. The others went hunting, and killed deer and turkeys. The Governor had graving irons, but could not grave anything, the stones were so hard. I graved my name on a tree by the river side; and the Governor buried a bottle, with a paper inclosed, on which he writ that he took possession of this place in the name and for King George the First of England.

"We had a good dinner and after it we got the men together and loaded all their arms, and we drank the King's health in champagne, and fired a volley—the Princess' health in Burgundy, and fired a volley, and all the rest of the Royal Family in claret, and fired a volley. We drank the Governor's health, and fired another volley."

After such a lavish expenditure of liquor and ammunition, the doughty knights rested on their arms for the remainder of the day. However, they were up at 7 A.M. on the morrow, recrossed the mountains, and headed for Germanna, whence they had set out. A number of bears were slain en route. One of them turned on the man who was pursuing him, tore the saddle-bags from his horse, and would have killed him, if other men and several dogs had not rushed to the rescue. Fontaine records that "we eat part of one of the bears, which tasted very well, and would be good, and might pass for veal, if one did not know what it was." After consuming the bear meat, he says that "we were very merry, and diverted ourselves with our adventures."

On September 10 the party reached Germanna. Spotswood, Fontaine, and a few others continued on to Williamsburg, the colonial capital, where they arrived on September 17.

The manner in which the participants in the expedition came to be known as Knights of the Golden Horseshoe was set forth in 1724 by Hugh Jones, as follows:

"For this expedition they were obliged to provide a great quantity of horseshoes (things seldom used in the lower parts of the country, where there are few stones) upon which account the Governor, upon their return, presented each of his companions with a golden horseshoe (some of which I have seen studded with valuable stones, resembling the heads of nails), with this inscription on the one side: Sic juvat transcendere montes; and on the other is written the tramontane order.

"This he did to encourage gentlemen to venture backwards, and make discoveries and new settlements; any gentleman being entitled to wear this golden horseshoe that can prove having drunk His Majesty's health upon Mount George." (Mount George is the mountain at Swift Run Gap, from which the expedition looked down upon the Shenandoah Valley.)

Such, in brief are the circumstances surrounding the explorations carried out by these adventurous pioneers 213 years ago. Their flagons of Burgundy and champagne, and their jewel-studded horseshoes have long since disappeared, but posterity recognizes that their discovery of the Shenandoah Valley was the first of that long series of thrusts into the Virginia wilderness which ultimately resulted in the opening up of the entire continent.

Others Preceded Spotswood to Valley

Three weeks ago the writer published an article concerning Governor Alexander Spotswood and his Knights of the Golden Horseshoe. Those who chanced to read it will recall that this swashbuckling crew, sustained by vast quantities of whiskey, wine, brandy, rum, champagne, punch, and other tipples, entered the Virginia wilderness in 1716, proceeded westward as far as Swift Run Gap in the Blue Ridge, and descending the mountains on the farther side, reached Elkton on the Shenandoah River. After describing their arrival at the gap, and their looking down upon the Shenandoah Valley below them, the writer said in his article of

September 1: "They were almost certainly the first white men who had ever gazed upon the scene."

This assertion was based upon the authority of the late W. W. Scott, sometime State Librarian and State Law Librarian, who says in his *History of Orange County*, published in 1907: "There is no reason to doubt and every reason to believe, that this crossing of the Blue Ridge was made in 1716 and was almost certainly the first that had ever been made by any body of white men."

But there are always erudite persons lying in wait to pounce upon the unwary writer when errors, large or small, creep into his copy, and the present case was no exception. Shortly after the article in question appeared, I was politely but firmly informed that my assertion that the Knights of the Golden Horseshoe were probably the first white men who had ever "gazed upon the scene" would have been accurate if it hadn't been for the fact that certain other white men had gazed upon it nearly half a century, and perhaps as much as eighty-four years, prior to 1716.

That is, they had gazed upon some portion of the Shenandoah Valley. And they undoubtedly had. It still appears probable, however, that Spotswood and his entourage were the first to look down upon the valley from Swift Run Gap, on what is now the Greene-Rockingham county line, so that my statement may have been technically accurate after all. Be that as it may, the purpose of the present article is to outline briefly the outstanding facts relative to the first expeditions into the Shenandoah Valley, and the early settlements there.

The Knights of the Golden Horseshoe were of the opinion that they were the discoverers of the valley, and this opinion appears to have been held pretty generally until recent years, but it is now known to be incorrect.

Dr. Philip Alexander Bruce, eminent historian of the Colonial period, is of the opinion that "the first white persons to gaze upon the paradise of the Great Valley were quite probably the indomitable Jesuit missionaries, for its outlines are to be found traced on their famous map, drafted in 1632."

Virgil A. Lewis, historian and archivist for the State of West Virginia, who did extensive research on the question, declares that a party of explorers, led by John Lederer, a German in the service of Governor William Berkeley, reached the crest of the Blue Ridge near Harper's Ferry in 1670, forty-six years ahead of Spotswood, and looked down upon the northern end of the valley from that point. This party included Lederer, Captain Collett, and nine Englishmen. It left the York River, passed the source of the Rappahannock, and finally attained the summit of the Blue Ridge.

Mr. Lewis also states that Governor Berkeley commissioned Colonel Abram Wood in the same year "for ye finding out of ye ebbing and flowing of ye water on ye other side of ye mountains." Wood accordingly sent out a party of five men, headed by Captain Thomas Batts, in 1671. They journeyed westward from the site of the present Petersburg, crossed the mountains, apparently at some point in what is now Craig County, and descended into what is now Monroe County, West Virginia. Pressing onward, they came to the canyons on New River, and soon afterward discovered the falls of the Great Kanawha, where they "had a sight of a curious river, like the Thames at Chelsea, but had a fall that made a great noise." Of course this exploration could hardly be said to have a direct bearing upon the discovery of the Shenandoah Valley, as the expedition passed below the southern end of the valley without touching it.

Those who wish the Knights of the Golden Horseshoe to have the credit for the discovery of the Shenandoah Valley may possibly question the evidence which supports the statement that Lederer and his party saw the valley forty-six years before Spotswood, but they certainly cannot question the fact that there is in Old Ronemus graveyard, Charles Town, West Virginia, a grave dated 1707. It is the grave of Catherine Bierlin, and the gravestone is of such value to historical students that it has been removed to the West Virginia Department of History and Archives at Charleston.

Charles Town, where she lies buried, is, of course, at the northern end of the valley, almost at Harper's Ferry, where the Shenandoah flows into the Potomac. It is in West Virginia, but it ought to be in Virginia. The people of Berkeley and Jefferson counties, at the upper end of the Shenandoah Valley, forming the extremity of the West Virginia "panhandle," were strongly sympathetic toward the Confederacy, and furnished an extraordinarily high percentage of their population to the Confederate armies. Jefferson County, in fact, claims to have furnished a greater percentage than any county in Virginia.

Yet these two counties, entitled by every consideration to remain in the Old Dominion, were arbitrarily taken away during the sixties, and included within the boundaries of West Virginia. Geographically they should belong to Virginia, for they form the northern end of the valley of the Shenandoah River. By sentiment and tradition they should be with Virginia, for they were overwhelmingly with the South in the War Between the States.

This, however, is a digression from the main topic. The Valley of Virginia, as set forth above, was discovered in 1670, if not in 1632 or earlier. In 1716 other explorers entered it about a hundred miles farther to the south. Then in 1725, John Van Meter, an Indian trader from the Hudson River, traversed the lower Shenandoah, upper Potomac, and South Branch valleys, but during all this period there seems to have been no permanent home in the Shenandoah Valley—that is, unless Catherine Bierlin and those who came with her established one.

But it is known that an individual bearing the strange name of Morgan Morgan built a home in 1726 on the site of the present village of Bunker Hill, in Berkeley County. He came to Virginia from Pennsylvania and to Pennsylvania from Wales. Shortly afterward he was followed by a group of German settlers who founded the present town of Shepherdstown, calling it "New Mecklenburg," after the German province from which they had come.

Settlers then began entering the valley fairly rapidly from that end. Among those who arrived around 1734 were Robert Harper, William Stroop, Thomas and William Forester, Van Swearingen, James Foreman, Edward Lucas, Jacob Hite, Jacob Lemon, Richard Mercer, Edward Mercer, Jacob Van Meter, Robert Stockton, Robert Buckles, John Taylor, Samuel Taylor, and John Wright. All these settled in what are now Berkeley and Jefferson counties.

At the other end of the valley, settlers were also beginning to filter in. Benjamin Borden, agent of Lord Fairfax, secured from

Governor Gooch the right to sue out a patent to 500,000 acres, chiefly in the modern county of Rockbridge, on the condition that he bring 100 families in to inhabit the land. He fulfilled this condition by 1737, the families being mainly Scotch-Irish. In 1736 William Beverley and others acquired a grant to 110,000 acres, located in the present county of Augusta, and this tract also was settled by Scotch-Irish.

Thus began the settlement of the Shenandoah Valley. With immigrants pouring into it at both ends, the entire area from Lexington to Harper's Ferry became populated to a more or less degree in a comparatively short time. Credit for the discovery of this fertile region, rich in history and romance, has for centuries been generally accorded to the Knights of the Golden Horseshoe, but, as set forth above, the first white men to find it seem to have been either the early Jesuits of three centuries ago, or John Lederer and his fellow adventurers.

Beginning of a Revolution
(1971)

Governor Dunmore's exultation over the victory at Point Pleasant was tempered by his concern over the provocative actions of the colonials at the Continental Congress. He was anxious to call the Virginia General Assembly into session, but uneasy as to what might happen if he did so. The result was that he issued several calls but each time changed his mind. He finally fixed on May 1775 as the date for the session, but by then the defiant actions of the Virginia Convention in St. John's Church, Richmond, and the reverberating fusillades at Lexington and Concord had taken matters out of his hands.

The convention which met in St. John's in March 1775 did so at the behest of Peyton Randolph, who had been empowered to issue the call. Richmond was chosen over Williamsburg as being less amenable to pressure from Dunmore. As early as the previous November, Patrick Henry had confided to friends that he believed war with England was inevitable. While this opinion was by no means general at the time, the convention met in the little church overlooking the James in an atmosphere of tension, if not apprehension. Small as St. John's was—much smaller than it is today—it was the largest building in the sprawling little town.

The delegates, among whom were practically all the great Virginians of that revolutionary generation, including six of the seven future signers of the Declaration of Independence, tied their horses in or near the churchyard. Some had ridden for days, even a week, over primitive roads and trails.

From *Virginia: The New Dominion* (Garden City, N.Y.: Doubleday and Co., 1971).

Peyton Randolph was in the chair, by unanimous vote. He put the affairs of the recent Continental Congress first on the agenda. After two days of reports and discussions, the delegates approved the decisions reached at Philadelphia.

When one or two other matters had been attended to, Patrick Henry was recognized. He offered a resolution declaring that:

"A well regulated militia . . . is the natural strength and only security of a free government. . . .

"Resolved, therefore, That this colony be immediately put into a posture of defense . . ."

Similar resolutions calling for a trained militia had been passed in other colonies, so there was nothing inherently revolutionary in this proposal. Yet George Washington, Edmund Pendleton, and other patriotic conservatives regarded the statement as unduly provocative and tantamount to a prophecy of war.

But Patrick Henry was not to be silenced. Rising in his pew, he began in a moderate tone, as was his wont. His carefully chosen words were those of a man reared on the near-frontier, yet by cultivated parents who stood well in the society of that day. His Scottish-born father was not only a judge and a former teacher but he had studied for four years at King's College, Aberdeen, and was knowledgeable in the classics. His mother, Sarah Winston, was of a good family. Patrick himself had read Virgil and Livy before he was fifteen, although like most of his contemporaries, he had apparently read relatively few books.

So when the Revolution's greatest orator began his immortal deliverance, he was speaking from a background of reading and culture which many today are unaware he possessed.

As he warmed to his subject, the strangely indefinable quality of his voice, so often mentioned by his contemporaries, seemed to hold his hearers enthralled. Finally he almost lifted them out of their seats with his blood-tingling climax:

"The war is actually begun! The next gale that sweeps from the North will bring to our ears the clash of resounding arms! Our brethren are already in the field! Why stand we here idle? . . . Is life so dear, or peace so sweet as to be purchased at the price of chains and slavery? Forbid it, Almighty God! I know not what course others may take, but as for me, give me liberty, or give me death!"

The "Tongue of the Revolution" had inspired his listeners with flaming words—words which were to reverberate throughout the colonies, beyond the seas, and far down the centuries. Those who heard Patrick Henry on March 23, 1775, remembered the occasion all their lives. "Let me be buried at this spot!" exclaimed Edward Carrington, who was listening through a window. His wish was granted more than a third of a century later.

When the stunned convention had gathered its wits, Richard Henry Lee, whose aristocratic profile resembled that of an ancient Roman senator, rose to second Henry's resolution. Lee's was a more elegant mode of speech than Henry's, his diction more polished, his voice smoother and more mellifluous, but the impact of his words was less overwhelming. Lee's gestures were flawless, despite the fact that he kept his left hand wrapped in a black silk handkerchief to hide the loss of its fingers in a hunting accident.

Thomas Jefferson, whose talents as a speaker were modest, at best, also spoke in favor of Henry's resolution.

It passed by a small majority. Henry was named chairman of the committee to put the colony in a posture of defense, with Lee as vice-chairman.

These events caused Governor Dunmore to become gravely concerned. He ordered British sailors to seize the powder in the powder horn at Williamsburg, and they carried off a wagonload. Whereupon the militia turned out, intent on marching to the Palace and seizing the governor. They were restrained by cooler heads when His Lordship promised to return the powder.

There were rumblings in the countryside, and horsemen gathered at Fredericksburg, with a view to marching on the capital. They were barely restrained by Peyton Randolph. Patrick Henry then led a group of Hanover County militia toward Williamsburg. They were joined en route by others from New Kent and King William, determined either to obtain £330 in compensation for the embezzled powder or to bring the powder back by main force. Dunmore was thrown into such a state of perturbation, if not panic, by these tidings, that the £330 was produced before the militia reached Williamsburg. The governor thereupon pronounced Henry an outlaw.

News of the fighting at Lexington and Concord during the previous month had finally reached Virginia. "The Sword is now drawn," said the *Virginia Gazette*, "and God knows when it will be sheathed."

It was early May, and the Second Continental Congress was convening in Philadelphia. The Virginia delegation was the same as at the first Congress—Randolph, Washington, Henry, Lee, Pendleton, Harrison, and Bland. The "shot heard 'round the world," fired in Massachusetts shortly before, had greatly heightened the tension, and there was much more excitement than there had been at the first Congress. This was also a much harder-working group, with far less attention given to merrymaking and conviviality.

Peyton Randolph, as usual, had been chosen unanimously as president, but he deemed it necessary to return to Virginia on May 24 to preside over the House of Burgesses which had been called into special session. Jefferson replaced him in the Virginia delegation at Philadelphia. John Hancock of Massachusetts was named to preside over the Continental Congress in Randolph's stead. The portly, overweight Randolph, back in Philadelphia, that autumn, died of a stroke.

George Washington was elected unanimously by the Congress to command the Continental Army. John and Samuel Adams were chiefly responsible for his election. The two New Englanders felt that the choice of a Virginian, as representing the largest and most populous colony, would tend to promote unity. They were also impressed by Washington's ability and character, although the austere Virginian was not described by anyone in the Congress as possessing "superlative military qualities." Washington, recognizing that his combat experience was limited to the command of a regiment in the French and Indian War some sixteen years before, was keenly aware of his deficiencies. But his sense of duty compelled him to accept. He insisted on serving without pay, and would take only his expenses.

His strong feeling of inadequacy and deep pessimism is seen in the remark he made, with tears in his eyes, to Patrick Henry: "Remember, Mr. Henry, what I now tell you: from the day that I enter upon the command of the American armies, I date my fall and the ruin of my reputation."

For the next five years, General Washington was to be engaged in leading the fight against the British in the northeast. The theater of operations would not move to Virginia again until 1779, and Washington himself would not be in command there until 1781.

But let us return to events in Virginia in May 1775. The burgesses learned soon after they had convened that Governor Dunmore had fled to the British man-of-war *Fowey*, anchored in the York River. After transacting some necessary business, the burgesses invited His Lordship to attend the usual legislative exercises in Williamsburg, but he insisted they join him on board the *Fowey*. They refused. When the burgesses adjourned on June 20, 1775, they terminated the long service of that lawmaking agency which had begun in 1619. It would be superseded ere long by the legislative body which we know today.

Dunmore remained aboard the *Fowey*, and then departed for Norfolk, after the erudite Richard Bland had made the somewhat drastic suggestion that he be hanged. At Norfolk, Dunmore was less unwelcome than at Williamsburg, for as Thomas J. Wertenbaker writes in his history of that port, Norfolk "was a thing apart from the rest of Virginia." As the colony's chief seaport and largest city, with six thousand inhabitants, it was cosmopolitan in population and outlook. And while leading citizens there exhibited the same standards of culture and civilized living as other Virginians in Tidewater, the milieu was urban rather than rural. Since most of the port's business was done with Great Britain, through Scottish merchants living in the town, Tory sentiment was stronger.

With Dunmore in flight, the Virginia convention which met in July decided to put the colony on a war footing. Two regiments of troops were to be raised and the militia were to be revitalized. A Committee of Safety was created, with Edmund Pendleton as chairman.

Powder Magazine, Williamsburg

Jamestown Island

Site of battlefield, Great Bridge

Waterfront at Norfolk

Where Merrimac and Monitor *clashed*, Hampton Roads

View of Gwynn's Island, from Mathews County

Mount Vernon, seen from the south

Monument to Mount Vernon slaves

This Committee of Safety was "the most powerful body that had ever exercised executive authority in Virginia," says David Mays in his biography of Pendleton. It could meet when and where it pleased, and "wield almost dictatorial power over both the sword and purse of the colony." It would discharge these functions until the next Virginia convention met.

Actual hostilities with the British got under way when Captain Squire of the British sloop of war *Otter* began raiding plantations along the Chesapeake. He appears to have carried off chickens as well as slaves. There was some sporadic rifle fire from a point on shore near Hampton, and two Britons were killed.

At the same time, a virtual blockade was instituted against Norfolk by patriotic county committees, while Dunmore remained aboard his flotilla in the harbor.

Dunmore landed a small force and seized a printing press which had been issuing revolutionary material. This gave the people of Norfolk such concern that perhaps one-third of the population either left for the interior or sailed for Britain.

Dunmore and the forces controlled by the Committee of Safety got into a minor skirmish near Kempsville, county seat of Princess Anne. The small British contingent of regulars won an easy victory over the disorganized colonials. In fact, Colonel Joseph Hutchings of the colonials was captured in a swamp by two Negro slaves who were fighting on the side of the British. There were to be other such feats by Negro soldiers and sailors in the Revolution, some of which have been overlooked by historians.

The easy British victory at Kempsville caused certain Norfolkians to conclude that it would be the part of wisdom to swear allegiance to Great Britain. Revolutionary patriots in Isle of Wight retaliated by tarring and feathering several leading loyalists.

Dunmore thereupon thought to make a ten-strike by proclaiming freedom for all slaves and indentured servants who would join his forces. This was felt by the colonials to be tantamount to inciting a slave insurrection, and it infuriated and alarmed the revolutionary leaders.

The Committee of Safety, under Pendleton, decided to move against Dunmore with the Second Regiment, under the command of Colonel William Woodford. Patrick Henry, colonel of the First Regiment, but without military experience, was thus passed over. Pendleton and Henry had been at odds on various issues, but the former's decision in favor of Woodford appears justified. Henry resigned his commission and returned to civil life, which may well have been in his own best interest.

Colonel Woodford was not only a veteran soldier, but he commanded a regiment of hardened fighters, many of whom wore hunting shirts with the legend "Liberty or Death!" and carried tomahawks and scalping knives. Dunmore, flushed with his easy victory at Kempsville, and unaware of the caliber of the opponents he now faced, decided to attack Woodford at Great Bridge, on the southern branch of the Elizabeth River, near Norfolk. He assembled perhaps six hundred troops, including all his regulars, sixty Tories, a couple of hundred Negroes, now known as the Ethiopian Corps, and a few sailors.

The Americans were entrenched behind breastworks, and they waited until the attackers came within fifty yards. At that point their sharpshooters opened up and mowed down the assaulting force. The latter fell back in disorder. On arriving in Norfolk, they rowed out to their ships. Tory families in the town made haste to follow them, beyond the reach of the enraged patriots.

Two Negroes rendered valiant service to the Americans in the Great Bridge engagement. William Flora, a free Negro from Portsmouth, was the last sentinel to leave his post as the enemy approached, and he withdrew "amidst a shower of musket balls," returning fire eight times. A slave belonging to Thomas Marshall, father of the future Chief Justice, crossed into the British lines, according to Colonel Woodford, and duped the British into thinking that Great Bridge fort was lightly manned and its defenders' morale low.

Despite his humiliating reverse, Dunmore once more assumed a threatening posture. He indicated that a general bombardment of Norfolk by his warships was imminent. Whereupon a large percentage of the population decided to leave at once, by whatever means were available, taking with them such possessions as they could. Shortly thereafter, on January 1, 1776, the four British vessels standing offshore opened up with all their guns. British sailors rowed ashore and set fire to warehouses and other buildings on the waterfront. American soldiers, many of whom regarded Norfolk as a nest of Tories, proceeded to help matters along by systematically putting the torch to much of the city, and looting on a wholesale scale. Over nine hundred houses, more than two-thirds of the entire community, were destroyed. The innocent suffered along with the guilty. It was midwinter and shelter was not only extremely scarce but food and water were equally so. Smallpox broke out, adding to the misery.

The American commanders decided in February to evacuate Norfolk, but the Virginia Convention was determined to leave nothing there which might be useful to the British. It ordered the remaining 416 houses burned. Nothing was left of the city but "complete desolation, charred timbers, blackened foundations, ashes." Citizens who were able to prove their allegiance to the Revolution were given compensation for their staggering losses, but the amounts were far from adequate. It would be several years before the community could recover from this disaster. Norfolk suffered perhaps more severely than any city in America during the Revolution.

Despite everything, there remained a staunch band of Norfolk patriots who carried on the fight for freedom. And in the late years of the eighteenth century the courage and fortitude of the Norfolkians again asserted themselves. Once the war was over, the city recovered rapidly, and resumed its place as a thriving seaport.

After the destruction of Norfolk, Dunmore was harassed by the eccentric Major General Charles Lee, who had been given temporary command of all Virginia forces. Lee's long green trousers, called "sherry-vallies," and the fact that he had a virtual herd of dogs which shared his bedroom, made him an object of considerable curiosity. He fired on Dunmore's ships from the shore. Shortly thereafter the governor, his noxious and germ-laden vessels crowded with runaway Tories and Negroes, sailed to Gwynn's Island, just off Gloucester County, and within range of its coastal batteries. Before long the redoubtable General Andrew Lewis, who had replaced Charles Lee in command of all Virginia forces on General Washington's recommendation—Lee having been transferred to Charleston, South Carolina—opened fire with a heavy cannonade against the British flotilla. Dunmore was unable to stand the punishment. He upped anchor and left Virginia forever. When the American forces landed on Gwynn's Island next day they viewed a shocking spectacle. The shore was strewn with corpses, and persons half-dead, victims of either the bombardment or of the smallpox and jail fever that had broken out on Dunmore's crowded and filthy ships.

The British governor's permanent departure in July 1776 ended until 1779 any serious threat of significant military activities against Virginia. But the colony was faced with many domestic wartime problems, and it had to put itself in a position to cope with possible attacks by land and sea.

Jack Jouett's Ride
(1961)

If you mean to be a historical figure, it is a good idea to get in touch with a leading literary figure—a Longfellow, a Homer, a Virgil. Paul Revere, Odysseus, Aeneas—they all took this precaution. Poor Captain Jack Jouett didn't. As a result this six-foot-four, two-hundred-pound giant from Virginia, who saved the leaders of the American Revolution from a disheartening and possibly disastrous reverse, has been left out of practically all the history books.

His forty-mile ride from Cuckoo Tavern to Monticello was one of the significant minor exploits of the struggle for independence. Unfortunately, it lacks a chronicler of adequate stature. Henry Wadsworth Longfellow, God rest his bones, put Revere on the map. He even gave us the exact hour at which Paul reached Concord on his "midnight ride," despite the fact that Revere himself says he was captured by the British before he got there. Jack Jouett's far longer and more perilous nocturnal dash across the Virginia countryside sorely needs a rousing ballad, preferably accurate as to facts, but comparable in popular appeal to the famous "Paul Revere's Ride."

Jouett's epochal exploit took place on the night of June 3–4, 1781, when the fortunes of the American colonists appeared far from prosperous. The traitor Benedict Arnold, by that time a British general, had been raiding and pillaging along the James from the river's mouth to Richmond, the Old Dominion's capital. General Cornwallis had detached his "hunting leopard," Lieutenant Colonel Banastre Tarleton, with 180 dragoons and 70 mounted

From *American Heritage*, December 1961.

infantrymen, to make a surprise march to Charlottesville, where the Virginia legislature was meeting following its flight from Richmond. His object was to capture Thomas Jefferson, author of that seditious document, the Declaration of Independence, and now governor of Virginia; Patrick Henry, whose "Give me liberty or give me death!" had sounded the call to arms six years before; and these signers of the Declaration: Richard Henry Lee, whose resolutions introduced in the Continental Congress in 1776 had led to adoption of the Declaration; Benjamin Harrison, ancestor of two future presidents; and Thomas Nelson, Jr., who had urged armed resistance to Great Britain in 1775 and had spent most of his fortune equipping soldiers for the Continental Army.

Tarleton's raid was as secret as he knew how to make it. He planned to cover the last seventy miles in twenty-four hours—an eighteenth-century blitzkrieg—and to pounce on Jefferson and the assemblymen unexpectedly. Valuable stores were also to be seized.

The British—many of whom were riding blooded horses seized on Virginia plantations—reached Cuckoo Tavern, Louisa County, on the evening of June 3. Up to that point, their movements had been successfully masked.

Here Jouett enters the picture. This twenty-seven-year-old native of Albemarle County was a captain in the Virginia militia, as were his three brothers, one of whom had been killed at Brandywine. Before the Revolution, the John Jouetts, father and son, had signed the Albemarle Declaration, whereby 202 residents of the county renounced allegiance to King George. And during the war, records show, "Commissary" John Jouett, Sr., sold considerable beef and other needed supplies from his Louisa County farm to the quartermasters of the Continental Army.

Jack Jouett may have been at or near Cuckoo Tavern on the night of June 3 while attending to his father's interests in that vicinity. At all events, Thomas Jefferson wrote years after, the young militiaman saw the British dragoons "pass his father's house" in Louisa County, and immediately suspected their object.

It was about ten o'clock. At once Captain Jouett leapt upon his thoroughbred, resolved to dash for Monticello and Charlottesville to warn the Assembly. He was forced to use a seldom-traveled route, for the British were on the main highway. Even the best roads of that era, with their ruts, mudholes, and thank-you-ma'ams, would be considered virtually impassable today; the difficulties that confronted this lone horseman on his all-night ride over backwoods byways can only be imagined.

The distance from Cuckoo Tavern to Charlottesville is about forty miles. The terrain, embracing parts of Louisa and Albemarle counties, is rolling and hilly. (It is in Louisa that the traveler from Tidewater first glimpses, on the far side of Albemarle, the soft contours of the Blue Ridge Mountains.) The moon was nearly full that night, but we do not know whether clouds obscured it. Even in bright moonlight, Jack Jouett was risking serious if not fatal injury in using this almost pathless route. As he rode through the woods and undergrowth of a virtual wilderness, his face was cruelly lashed and scarred.

Meanwhile Tarleton, by his own account, halted his troopers at 11 P.M. on a plantation near Louisa Courthouse. After resting for three hours, they set out again at 2 A.M. Not long thereafter they encountered a train of eleven wagons loaded with arms and clothing for General Nathanael Greene's Continental troops in South Carolina. They burned the wagon train instead of taking it with them, Tarleton wrote, in order that no time might be lost.

Soon after daybreak the expedition reached Castle Hill, home of the celebrated Dr. Thomas Walker, the explorer, and nearby Belvoir, home of his son, John. "Some of the principal gentlemen of Virginia . . . were taken out of their beds," Tarleton wrote. "Part were paroled . . . while others were carried off." There was a "halt of half an hour" to refresh the horses, he added, after which the troops moved on toward Charlottesville.

Various legends have grown up around this halt at Castle Hill. The principal one says that Dr. Walker craftily offered Tarleton an elaborate breakfast, the consumption of which so delayed the Briton that Jack Jouett was able to beat him to Monticello and Charlottesville. Another legend has British dragoons stealing, one after another, two breakfasts which had been prepared for their commander and Dr. Walker telling Tarleton that he would have to post a guard on the kitchen if he desired nourishment. This was done, the story continues, and the cook and attendant flunkies finally served the third breakfast to the Colonel intact. But by the time he had eaten it, Jefferson and most of the legislature had escaped. There are even some ridiculous references in one modern account to "potent mint juleps, Sally Lunn and waffles."

If breakfast *was* consumed at Castle Hill by any Briton in the early morning of June 4, 1781, we may be reasonably sure that there was no such menu as this. Aside from the fact that mint juleps and other such sybaritic provender at so early an hour seem absurd under the circumstances, Tarleton would hardly have been stupid enough to fall into so obvious a trap. His own statement that he halted only half an hour at Castle Hill to rest his horses impresses one as far more authentic, although his account may have shortened the actual time somewhat in order not to appear lacking in zeal.

While Tarleton and his men were tarrying at Castle Hill, Jouett was riding through the dawn toward Monticello. His route took him to the Rivanna River ford at the hamlet of Milton. A few miles farther on, he made the ascent to Jefferson's stately mansion, arriving at about 4:30 A.M., several hours ahead of the British; their relatively brief halt at Walker's estate cannot have been responsible for their failure to bag Jefferson and the other patriots.

On reaching Monticello, Jouett proceeded at once to rouse the sleeping occupants. Among them, besides Jefferson, were the Speaker and other members of the two houses of the General Assembly. Jefferson not only thanked Jouett for his timely warning but is understood to have tendered a bracing glass or two of his best Madeira. Refreshed, the rider mounted his horse and rode the remaining two miles to Charlottesville, where he awakened dozens more of the snoring solons.

Jefferson and his guests had been far from panic-stricken by the tidings. They "breakfasted at leisure," Jefferson afterward wrote;

then the guests joined their colleagues in town. Jefferson, remaining behind at Monticello, made arrangements to send his wife and children to Enniscorthy, the Coles estate fourteen miles distant, via Blenheim, the Carter estate. He then spent nearly two hours securing his important papers.

Suddenly Captain Christopher Hudson, en route to join Lafayette's forces, arrived at a gallop to say that British troopers were ascending the mountain to Monticello. Jefferson sent his family off at once in their carriage but was himself in no great hurry to depart. He tied his horse at a point on the road between Monticello and Carter's Mountain, and through his telescope scanned the Charlottesville streets. Seeing no signs of unwonted activity, and hearing no approaching hoofbeats on the mountainside, he started back to Monticello for a few last-minute arrangements. He soon noticed, however, that he had dropped his light "walking sword," and returned to pick it up. He focused his telescope for a final look toward the town and was startled to see British dragoons, in their green uniforms faced with white, and mounted infantrymen, wearing red, swarming in the streets.

Instantly Jefferson leaped upon his horse and plunged into the woods. The British were already at Monticello: he had made the narrowest sort of escape. He eluded Tarleton's men, and joined his family later in the day for dinner at Blenheim.

Tarleton himself did not go to Monticello but remained in Charlottesville. He gave strict orders to Captain McLeod, commander of the detachment he was sending to capture Jefferson, not to damage the house in any way. An account handed down in the family, and accepted by Henry S. Randall, Jefferson's mid-nineteenth-century biographer, has it that when the British suddenly hove into view on the mountaintop, Martin, Jefferson's Negro body servant, was passing silver and other articles to Caesar, another slave, through a trap door in the wooden floor of the portico. As the dragoons burst upon the scene, Martin dropped the trap door, leaving Caesar in total darkness. He remained there, quiet and uncomplaining, until the raiders left some eighteen hours later. Apparently they need not have feared: except for the pilferage of a few articles in the cellar, McLeod's men carried out their instructions.

By contrast, the main body of General Cornwallis's army, which Tarleton joined next day at Elk Hill, Jefferson's plantation at Point of Fork (now Columbia), wrought devastation far and wide. Not content with burning the barns, destroying the crops, taking the horses and cattle, and cutting the throats of the young colts, Cornwallis even carried off thirty Negroes. He herded them in with other slaves who were suffering from smallpox and "putrid fever," and most of them died.

In Charlottesville, meanwhile, the General Assembly was hurriedly taking its departure. The members had convened hastily on getting the word from Jouett that the British were coming and had adjourned at once, resolving to meet three days later at Staunton, forty miles to the west beyond the mountains.

Tarleton was so close on their heels that although Patrick Henry, Richard Henry Lee, Benjamin Harrison, Thomas Nelson, Jr., and numerous others got away, seven assemblymen were taken. One who managed to escape was General Edward Stevens, who was recuperating from a wound received at the Battle of Guilford Courthouse. Randall relates that Stevens was plainly dressed and mounted on a shabby horse, whereas Jack Jouett, riding his thoroughbred, was dressed in "a scarlet coat and military hat and plume," for he "had an eccentric custom of wearing such habiliments." The British ignored Stevens, thinking he was a person of no importance, and went after Jouett, whose dress led them to believe him an officer of high rank. But the athletic, well-mounted Jouett was too fast for them, and made his getaway. General Stevens, meanwhile, had taken advantage of the diversion to disappear.

Thomas Jefferson's political opponents inside and outside the state tried to make it appear that he had behaved in a cowardly fashion at the time of Tarleton's raid. For many years thereafter his perennial enemies, the Federalists, sought to picture him as having fled ignominiously before the British. Tarleton himself wrote that Jefferson "provided for his personal safety with a precipitate retreat."

All this was grossly unfair. If anything, Jefferson waited too long at Monticello after being warned by Jouett, with the result that he barely escaped capture. Certainly he was no more to be criticized than the legislators, who beat a more "precipitate retreat" than he. As a matter of fact, when a group of them—including Henry, Harrison, and John Tyler, Sr.—stopped in a hut beyond Charlottesville, the old woman of the house proceeded to abuse them roundly for "running away." But when she found Henry was one of their number, she apologized.

What would have been the fate of such men as Jefferson, Henry, Harrison, Nelson, and Lee, if they had fallen into British hands? They would almost certainly have been carried off into captivity by Tarleton—just as he carried off several "gentlemen" taken at or near Castle Hill on the previous day; it is hardly conceivable that men of the stature of Jefferson, Henry, and the rest would have been paroled. Their capture would have been a serious blow to the morale of the Continentals, especially at a time when things were going rather badly for their cause. Incalculable, even catastrophic, results might have followed from such a coup.

The General Assembly of Virginia was deeply sensible of its debt to Jack Jouett, for a few days afterward, on June 15, it adopted the following resolution:

Resolved: That the executive be desired to present to Captain John Jouett an elegant sword and pair of pistols as a memorial of the high sense which the General Assembly entertain of his activity and enterprise in watching the motions of the enemy's cavalry on their late incursion to Charlottesville and conveying to the assembly timely information of their approach, whereby the designs of the enemy were frustrated and many valuable stores preserved.

Jouett was given the pistols in 1783, but it was twenty years before he received the "elegant sword." By that time he had made quite a name for himself beyond the Alleghenies, in present-day Kentucky.

His career there started out badly. According to a story handed down in the family, he and his companions were moving westward through the Cumberland Gap and along Daniel Boone's Wilderness Road when they heard the cries of a woman coming from a lonely cabin. On investigating, they found a man beating his wife. Jouett went gallantly to the lady's rescue and knocked her husband down. But the Virginian discovered at once that he who intervenes in such an intramural dispute incurs the wrath of both parties thereto: the lady reached for a long-handled frying pan and hit Jouett over the head so forcefully that the bottom of the pan was knocked out and the rim driven down over his neck. Not until he found a blacksmith, thirty-five miles down the road, was he able to disengage his head.

Undiscouraged, Jouett settled down in Mercer County and entered politics. He helped Kentucky break off from Virginia and become a sovereign state, served four terms in the new legislature, pioneered livestock breeding in Woodford County—in the bluegrass where today great racing stables raise swift colts for the Derby—and in his later years was the friend of Andrew Jackson, Henry Clay, and the great families of his adopted state. Among his numerous children was one of America's most noted portrait painters, Matthew Harris Jouett ("I sent Matthew to college to make a gentleman of him," said old Jack, "and he has turned out to be nothing but a damned sign painter"). Among Matthew's children was James Edward "Fighting Jim" Jouett, a distinguished naval officer, who seems to have shared his grandfather's fate in being forgotten by history. What Admiral Farragut reportedly said at the Battle of Mobile Bay was: "Damn the torpedoes! Four bells! Captain Drayton go ahead! Jouett full speed!" Alas, it is usually remembered by the average schoolboy as "Damn the torpedoes! Full speed ahead!"

By the time "Fighting Jim's" hour of glory struck, his grandfather was of course long since dead. And by the world forgotten: he was buried in the family cemetery at his Bath County farm, Peeled Oak, but the grave was unmarked, and it took a twentieth-century researcher, the late Mrs. Joel M. Cochran of Charlottesville, Virginia, to find the spot where the old Revolutionary hero was laid to rest.

Yes, Jack Jouett's ride from Cuckoo Tavern to Monticello cries out for a ballad that will seize the fancy of the American people.

The hoofbeats of his steed, toiling and sweating through the warm June night across forty miles of Virginia countryside, come echoing down the years. Jack Jouett gave some of America's greatest patriots a timely warning in one of the Revolution's dark hours, but his valorous deed has been well-nigh forgotten. He deserves a kinder fate.

George Washington's Boozing Gardener

(1932)

This piece for the Times-Dispatch *in 1932 is a memento of the campaign to outflank the "drys" and repeal the Eighteenth Amendment outlawing alcoholic beverages.*

Some eighteen months ago it was pointed out in this place that our dry friends have been trying to make a prohibitionist out of Thomas Jefferson. Attention was called to the fact that a character representing Jefferson appeared in the pageant presented by the Fifteenth International Congress Against Alcoholism at Washington in 1920, and that an effort was made to show that the Sage of Monticello would favor the Eighteenth Amendment if he were alive today. Extracts also were quoted from works of reference published by the professional drys in which an attempt was made to put the author of the Declaration of Independence and the Statute of Virginia for Religious Freedom in the same boat with Pussyfoot Johnson and Clarence True Wilson. An analysis of the claims of the drys relative to Jefferson was made by this writer in a series of three articles, and he showed, at least to his own satisfaction, that whereas Jefferson was at all times an advocate of temperance, he would never have countenanced the brand of prohibition we now enjoy.

But while the Anti-Saloon League and allied forces have made quite a drive to land Jefferson in the prohibitionist camp, they have not, so far as I am aware, made any overtures in the direction of

From the *Richmond Times-Dispatch*, February 21, 1932.

George Washington. That eminent distiller has thus far eluded their efforts, and it is doubtful that even Pussyfoot Johnson, who had to "lie, bribe and drink to put over prohibition in America," could unearth sufficient evidence to justify George's inclusion in the ranks of the moral forces.

There is, indeed, considerable evidence that the Father of His Country was on the other side of the fence. In addition to the fact that he consumed his share of vinous beverages and the further fact that he made large quantities of the stuff at Mount Vernon, there was that famous contract of his with his gardener, made in the year of our Lord, 1787. In view of the fact that tomorrow is Washington's natal day, indeed the 200th anniversary of his birth, it seems fitting to recall the terms of that famous state paper.

The gardener, whose name was Philip Barter, signed up with Washington for service at Mount Vernon in "articles of agreement made this twelfth day of April, Anno Domini, one thousand seven hundred and eighty-seven by and between George Washington, Esq., of the parish of Truro, in the county of Fairfax, State of Virginia, on the one part, and Philip Barter, gardener, on the other."

The gardener contracted to conduct himself soberly, diligently, and honestly, and promised "to the best of his knowledge and abilities, not at any time to suffer himself to be disguised by liquor except on times hereinafter mentioned."

The contract went on to provide that Phil might disguise himself with usquebaugh in the following manner and on the following occasions:

"In consideration of these things being well and truly performed on the part of said Philip Barter, the said George Washington doth agree to allow him (the said Philip) the same kind and quality of provisions he has heretofore had, and likewise, annually, a decent suit of clothes, befitting a man of his station . . . and four dollars at Christmas, with which he may be drunk four days and four nights; two dollars at Easter to effect the same purpose; two dollars at Whitsuntide to be drunk for two days; a dram in the morning and a drink of grog at dinner at noon."

In addition to the fact that this agreement not only obliterates any possibility that Washington might be considered one of prohibition's votaries, it also serves to dispel the illusion that he was any species of cast-iron saint with no human foibles and no sense of humor, a prissy fellow who said, "I cannot tell a lie, I did it with my little hatchet," and made himself generally offensive and obnoxious. The sooner people get rid of these notions about Washington and discover that he had his frailties and weaknesses like the rest of us, that he cussed like a trooper and drank whiskey when he felt so inclined, the better for all concerned.

But the contract which he signed with Barter also induces this reflection: What sort of a bender could a man get on with only $4 to last him four days and four nights? Either the gardener had a very limited capacity or $4 would purchase more firewater than it does now. Doubtless the latter explanation is the correct one. Prices were not only lower then than at present, but Barter was doubtless able to get a reduced rate at the Mount Vernon still. Hence it is reasonable to suppose that despite his limited finances he found it possible to remain satisfactorily stewed for four days and nights in the vicinity of Yuletide, as well as for some forty-eight hours at Whitsuntide and Easter, in accordance with the agreement.

The fact that George Washington, who seems to be regarded by most persons as the greatest man America has produced, was not inclined to interfere with the drinking habits of his fellow citizens or even of his employees should be recalled at this time, particularly in view of legislation on this subject pending at the current session of the General Assembly.

The Father of His Country would be gratified to note the trend in the legislature of his native state, for the solons seem to be awakening at last to the realization that the prohibition law is somewhat less sacred than revealed religion. Some noteworthy steps have been taken in the direction of sanity at the session now in progress, and while there is no assurance that the good work will not be undone before adjournment, there have been unmistakable indications already that the moral forces are less potent than of yore.

Take the action of the House Committee on Moral and Social

Welfare in reporting by unanimous vote the Page bill reducing fees in prohibition cases to the level of fees in other criminal cases, where such fees are paid to the state, and also lightening in a marked degree the penalty for transporting less than a half a gallon, where liquid refreshments are for personal use, rather than for sale. This committee is not packed with depraved young men from the cities; on the contrary, more than half of the members are from rural constituencies. Yet without a dissenting voice, this body recommended leveling the fees in dry law cases, and abolishing the jail sentence, now compulsory, for transporting, where the amount is less than half a gallon and is for personal use. The bill which it approved also provides that automobiles shall not be confiscated in such cases, whereas at present every car caught with anything containing more than one-half of 1 percent is immediately seized. It need hardly be said that five years ago no such bill as this would have been reported out at all, much less by a unanimous vote.

Or take the action of the House of Delegates in decapitating the four special prosecutors heretofore employed by the state for the purpose of supplementing the activities of commonwealth's attorneys in prohibition cases. Here again no one can say what will happen when the Senate gets hold of this bill. The four may not stay decapitated. The fact remains, however, that this has been done by the House, a body of men coming largely from rural constituencies. It would have been unthinkable a few years ago, depression or no depression.

Other legislation liberalizing the dry laws is now pending in one branch or the other of the Assembly, but the action already taken in the instances mentioned serves to illustrate the trend. It is a happy omen on the 200th anniversary of George Washington's birth. That great man, it is safe to say, would rejoice if he could rise from his cerements at Mount Vernon and see the legislature of his native state freeing itself gradually from the bondage of ecclesiasticism.

He Made the Court Supreme
(1955)

A tall, ungainly, sloppily dressed man loitered on the fringes of Richmond's market one day in the early 1800s, when a stranger approached with a newly bought turkey. The stranger offered him a small coin to carry the bird home. The unkempt character thereupon took the turkey and walked behind the stranger to the latter's abode. Upon arrival, he collected the coin and left.

But our seedy-looking friend was no ignorant yokel. He was John Marshall, Chief Justice of the United States, who was having his little joke—as he often did. Richmond almost split its sides over the episode.

Jovial, approachable, absent-minded John Marshall was, in fact, two different people. He was the "life of the party" at social gatherings, a connoisseur of Madeira, an expert at quoits, a quipster who could toss off a rhyme on the spur of the moment, and who always dressed badly and hated stiffness and formality in his private relationships. Yet he was a person of immense dignity when sitting on the nation's highest tribunal, garbed in his robes of office, his black eyes flashing, his voice intoning one of his epochal judicial decisions. Had it not been for these decisions, the infant republic might not have survived its early stresses and strains.

John Marshall and his cousin, Thomas Jefferson, were both descended from William Randolph, of "Turkey Island," and his wife, Mary Isham, perhaps the most notable couple in American history, since their descendants also included "Light Horse Harry" Lee, John Randolph of Roanoke, and Robert E. Lee. But although Marshall and Jefferson were blood relations, they came to hate

From the *Saturday Evening Post*, September 24, 1955.

each other. Aligned in opposing political camps, they represented contrasting theories of government. Marshall, the Federalist, believed in a strong central authority; Jefferson, the Republican—as the Democrats then termed themselves—was our foremost advocate of state rights, individual liberty, and the freedom of the human mind. Each made a priceless contribution to the building of the nation.

Marshall's convictions as to the need for a strong national government stemmed from his experiences in the American Revolution. He fought bravely at Brandywine, Germantown, and Monmouth, and was at Valley Forge during the terrible winter of 1777–78. He was angered by the manner in which the thirteen bickering colonies refused to furnish badly needed men and supplies to the Continental Army, except when they found it convenient.

This situation was borne in upon him with redoubled force as he struggled beside the starving, freezing soldiers at Valley Forge. Captain-Lieutenant Marshall's invincible spirit rose above the horrors and privations of that icy winter in the snow-covered hills of Pennsylvania, and his sunny disposition did much to lift the spirits of his men. Diaries of his companions in arms tell of his good humor in the midst of death, disease, and want. He took part in the games which were improvised to while away the hours, and was the best athlete in his regiment.

John Marshall was born just 200 years ago on September 24, 1755, in a log cabin on the Virginia frontier in what is now Fauquier County. He was the eldest of fifteen children. While Indians were not a threat in the immediate neighborhood, the primeval forest was filled with bears and other game. Throughout his youth, his parents found it practically impossible to buy goods in stores, and the family generally wore homespun. Marshall's talented mother, whose maiden name was Mary Randolph Keith, used thorns instead of pins. His father, Thomas Marshall, a man of great ability and force, had no formal education. He served several terms in the Virginia House of Burgesses and held other important offices.

John Marshall and his father both enlisted in the Culpeper Minute Men at the outbreak of the Revolution, Thomas being given the rank of major and his nineteen-year-old son that of lieutenant. As a member of the Virginia Convention of 1775, the elder Marshall had heard Patrick Henry's flaming appeal for "liberty or death." Those fateful words were worked into the hunting shirts of the Culpeper Minute Men. Both Marshalls soon joined the Continental Army and served under General Washington for four years.

John Marshall was sent home at the end of 1779 because enlistments in the regiments in which he had commanded expired, and too many officers were therefore available. He waited in vain for a new command.

While waiting he went to Williamsburg to be with his father, who had become a state councilor. There the young captain met Mary Ambler, then only fourteen, and the two fell in love at first sight. Mary lost her heart to him, although he was universally regarded by the ladies as awkward and ill at ease, and his dress was as slovenly as it remained throughout his life.

George Wythe, the celebrated law professor, was lecturing at the College of William and Mary, and Marshall enrolled in his course. The young law student remained only six weeks. His notebook shows the name of Mary Ambler scrawled in many different places, indicating that his mind was on things other than his studies. Yet this six weeks' course was all the formal education, legal or otherwise, that John Marshall ever had. He had been tutored for two years by clergymen and the rest of the time by his parents.

When he left William and Mary and began the practice of law in Fauquier County, clients were slow in coming. He seized the opportunity to have himself vaccinated for smallpox, then a serious scourge. In order to do so, he had to go to Philadelphia, and since he had no other means of locomotion, he walked, averaging thirty-five miles a day. On his arrival he looked so disreputable that the tavern to which he applied refused to admit him. He finally obtained lodging elsewhere, was vaccinated—and walked back to Virginia.

Finding, on his return to Fauquier, that clients were still scarce, Marshall decided to offer for the state assembly. His campaign was successful. Mary Ambler's father had moved to Richmond as state treasurer, so Marshall was able to redouble the ardor of his suit when he arrived in the new capital to take his seat. He and Mary were married early in 1783.

Thus began one of the most beautiful love stories in our history. Mary Marshall—whose nickname was Polly—contracted a nervous affliction early in her married life, but this merely increased her husband's devotion. His idolatry was truly touching. Polly practically never wrote him, because of her malady, but he wrote her regularly whenever he was away from home, and in the most endearing terms. Ten children were born to them.

From the outset they lived in Richmond, and it was as a legislator representing that town that Marshall rendered his principal service in the Virginia Assembly. From the beginning he was a marked man. In 1782, when he was barely twenty-seven and serving his first term, he was chosen by his legislative colleagues as one of the eight members of the Council of State, the governor's cabinet.

After several terms in the lawmaking body, Marshall's conspicuous ability was recognized by all. His good humor and conviviality made him widely popular, and his grasp of public questions, especially legal ones, gave his views particular weight. When the Virginia Convention of 1788 met to consider ratification of the new federal Constitution, Marshall was elected a delegate.

Many of the great Virginians of that era were members of the convention. In that glittering assemblage, thirty-three-year-old John Marshall stood out as one of the most effective advocates of the Constitution. Virginia finally ratified it by a vote of 89 to 79.

Once the Constitution became the law of the land, Marshall felt that a long step forward had been taken toward strengthening the Union, but he was alarmed by certain prevailing tendencies. The rumblings of the French Revolution were growing louder, and Washington, Marshall, and the other Federalists became more and more disturbed by the outspoken sympathy shown in the United States for the revolutionaries. Marshall had had strong democratic leanings when he fought in the American Revolution, but only a few years later he had reached the melancholy conclusion that "man is incapable of governing himself." This, of course, was exactly contrary to the views of Jefferson and most of the other citizens of this country, who felt deep sympathy for the French people in their bloody uprising against a tyrannical king. But the passage of the years merely confirmed Marshall in his unfavorable opinion of popular government and majority rule.

By the time George Washington became the first president of the infant republic, John Marshall was recognized as one of the ablest Federalists in the United States. Washington tried in 1795 to persuade him to accept the post of attorney general, but Marshall had a large and growing family, and he felt it necessary to decline. The salary of the attorney general was only $1500.

Marshall had become the undisputed leader of the Richmond bar. He and his adored Polly were anxious to own a home which would be commensurate with his standing in the community. So in 1789 he had bought an entire tree-shaded block in an excellent residential section, and built thereon the comfortable brick dwelling which was to be his abode until his death forty-six years later. The house stands today just as it was when he lived there, although the outbuildings and grounds have long since disappeared. As Chief Justice, Marshall wrote some of his most famous opinions under the trees.

Three years after his home was finished, Marshall appeared, with Patrick Henry, as one of the defense counsel in connection with the notorious scandal involving Richard Randolph and Ann Cary Randolph, Richard's seventeen-year-old unmarried sister-in-law. Richard and Ann were tried in Cumberland Courthouse, Virginia, for the murder of Ann's infant child, of whom Richard was apparently the father. They were acquitted. Ann, usually called "Nancy," later married Gouverneur Morris, of New York, the statesman and diplomat. The trial at Cumberland Courthouse was one of the few criminal cases in which Marshall ever took part.

In the spacious dining room of his new Richmond residence he began giving his famous "lawyer dinners," to which the members of the bench and bar were invited. He was the liveliest person at these affairs, as he was on most other social occasions, and he filled the air with quips and jests.

An idea of his talent for "off-the-cuff" repartee is seen in his quick response when challenged in a Philadelphia club to use the word "paradox" in verse. Glancing through a door at several convivial Kentuckians, Marshall came up at once with

> In the Blue Grass region
> A paradox was born,
> The corn was full of kernels
> And the colonels full of corn.

A short time after he built his house in Richmond, Marshall joined with others in contracting to buy what was left of the vast Virginia estate of Lord Fairfax, embracing approximately 160,000 acres. Robert Morris, the Philadelphia capitalist, was to advance the money. But Morris went bankrupt, and the financial burden on Marshall became almost intolerable. Hence, when President John Adams offered him a remunerative appointment in 1797 as one of three special envoys to France, he accepted. Charles Cotesworth Pinckney, of South Carolina, and Elbridge Gerry, of Massachusetts, were the two others.

The mission was to seek adjustment of serious difficulties which had arisen between the United States and France. The latter country felt that we had broken our agreements, and that we were much too friendly with Great Britain.

The blood and terror of the French Revolution were things of the past, and Napoleon Bonaparte was beginning to set himself astride the continent of Europe. France was "feeling her oats," and was actually encouraging French privateers to seize American ships on the high seas. Several hundred of our vessels had been taken in this piratical fashion.

When the three American envoys arrived in Paris, they found that they had to deal with an oily individual named Talleyrand, an unfrocked priest who had spent two and a half years in exile in the United States. Talleyrand was then almost unknown, but he was soon to become France's foreign minister and the ablest diplomat in Europe.

The negotiations consisted mainly of efforts on the part of Talleyrand to squeeze a $250,000 bribe out of the Americans. Although Marshall had gone to Paris the least known and most inexperienced of the three envoys, he soon emerged as the strong man of the delegation. The bullying tactics of the French, who declared that Napoleon was about the invade England, and that we would be next, did not frighten him. Nor did threats of personal violence. As spokesman for the mission, he upheld American interests with dignity, courage, and honor.

This "XYZ Affair"—as it was called by virtue of the code used in connection with it by our government—was a great triumph for Marshall, and a crucial turning point in his career. Although he and his associates were unable to obtain an agreement in Paris, he returned a hero. He was accorded a magnificent welcome in Philadelphia, the capital—the greatest such welcome any American, except Washington, had ever received. It included a banquet at which the climactic toast was the famous "Millions for defense, but not one cent for tribute!"

Marshall cleared approximately $15,000 on his eleven-month mission to France, since he was paid nearly $20,000 and his expenses were not more than $5,000. Although this was applied to his personal indebtedness on the Fairfax estate, he still found himself badly strapped—so strapped, in fact, that he could not afford to accept an appointment to the Supreme Court when it was first tendered by President Adams in 1798.

A personal appeal from George Washington, however, did cause him to run for Congress. Although the Richmond district contained many more Republicans than Federalists, Marshall's great prestige and popularity won for him.

When he got to Congress he showed exceptional independence and integrity by voting contrary to his party's program on two major issues. He cast the deciding ballot in favor of repeal of the obnoxious section of the Sedition Law—a law favored by the Federalists which went to extreme lengths in attempting to prevent criticism of the national government, then in Federalist hands. He also ignored party discipline when he insisted on taking the teeth out of the Disputed Elections Bill, under the original terms of which the Federalists could have stolen the approaching presidential election.

Despite Marshall's unwillingness to bend under the party lash, President Adams tried to make him secretary of war. He declined. Then, in the spring of 1800, Adams persuaded him to accept the portfolio of secretary of state. No sooner had Marshall been sworn in than Adams left for Massachusetts to be with his ill wife. This left Marshall virtually in charge of the national government. Adams remained away until the fall, and Marshall had to sweat it out in Washington, the new capital. This metropolis was a town of some 3,000 persons, alternately muddy and dusty, surrounded by forests, swamps and bogs, and plagued by vast swarms of mosquitoes.

When his party lost the election of 1800, President Adams decided to appoint as many Federalist judges as possible before he went out of office. He offered the post of Chief Justice to Marshall, and the latter accepted. John Jay, the first incumbent, had declined reappointment on the ground that the position did not carry sufficient power and prestige. Marshall soon gave it both, by the force of his character and intellect.

Under the system then prevailing, Supreme Court justices had to ride the circuit, in addition to sitting in Washington. Mr. Justice Marshall had the grievous misfortune on one occasion to arrive in Raleigh, North Carolina, minus his trousers. With his usual absent-mindedness, he had neglected to bring them with him. He wrote his wife that he was without a pair of breeches for several days after his arrival, until he could find a "taylor," but did not explain what he had worn on the journey from Richmond. Presumably the judicial robes concealed his predicament while he was on the bench in Raleigh.

This piquant episode occurred in 1803, shortly before Marshall was to render the first of his series of precedent-making judicial opinions—that of *Marbury* v. *Madison*. The litigation grew out of Marshall's own negligence in forgetting to deliver a commission as justice of the peace to a man named William Marbury—a "midnight appointment" of President Adams in the last hours of his administration—and the subsequent determination of Secretary of State James Madison not to name Marbury to the post. Marshall seized upon this seemingly trivial case to assert the right of the Supreme Court to invalidate acts of Congress which conflict with the federal Constitution. Albert J. Beveridge says, in his monumental biography of Marshall, that "this principle is wholly and exclusively American," and "America's original contribution to the science of law."

Marbury had applied to the Supreme Court for a writ of mandamus under Section 13 of the Judiciary Act of 1789, to compel Secretary of State Madison to issue him his commission. The section empowered the court to issue such writs "in cases warranted by the principles and usages of law." But the Chief Justice took the position that the federal Constitution, in defining the original jurisdiction of the Supreme Court, did not include the issuance of writs to executive officers. He held, therefore, that it devolved upon the court to determine whether an act of Congress or the Constitution is paramount. Marshall ruled that "a legislative act contrary to the Constitution is not law."

This pronouncement enraged Jefferson and his party; for while they had won a minor victory, in that Marbury was denied his writ, they were infuriated when Marshall's decision sharply criticized Secretary of State Madison for withholding the commission, and termed Madison's action "a plain violation." They accordingly threatened the Chief Justice with impeachment. Not only so, but they actually set in motion impeachment proceedings against several federal judges, notably Associate Justice Samuel Chase, of the Supreme Court.

Justice Chase had been an unusually militant Federalist, and a few years before had actually directed a United States marshal to strike from a jury panel "any of those creatures or persons usually called democrats." The House of Representatives impeached him on charges of misfeasance and malfeasance. Chief Justice Marshall appeared as a witness for the defense at the Senate's trial of Chase. Marshall was evidently rattled by the violence of the assault on his colleague, and he made a poor impression. Chase, however, was finally acquitted, and this gave Marshall a feeling of greater security.

Already the great weight of Marshall's personality and intellect was bringing prestige and dignity to the nation's highest tribunal.

Immediately upon his appointment in 1801, he had become almost the sole mouthpiece of the court, and for the next eleven years he wrote practically all the opinions. Not only so, but there were scarcely any dissents, despite the fact that most of the other justices were members of the opposition party, and interparty feeling was running high. After 1812, Marshall continued to write the opinions in practically all cases involving constitutional questions, but several hundred opinions involving other issues were written by his fellow justices. Yet it was not only on constitutional questions that he was able to carry the other judges along with him despite their Republican affiliation; during the entire thirty-four years of his service as Chief Justice, he dissented only eight times. So remarkable an example of the domination of an able bench by the intellectual power and persuasive charm of one man would be hard to find.

During his early years on the court, Marshall owed large sums for his share of the Fairfax estate. His salary as Chief Justice was only $4000, and he had somehow to raise additional funds. This led him to write his five-volume *Life of Washington*. The work not only made far less money than its author expected but it also had a poor critical reception.

At about the time when Marshall finished this biography, the Burr conspiracy burst upon the nation. Aaron Burr, who had killed Alexander Hamilton in a duel a few years before, was suspected of strange plottings in the Southwest, even of a treasonable scheme to split the Union. This led to the greatest criminal trial in American history, with John Marshall presiding as part of his routine duties on the circuit bench.

The bitter antagonism between Jefferson and Marshall neared its climax during this trial, which took place in the capitol at Richmond. President Jefferson was convinced that Burr was guilty, and he did his best to obtain a conviction. Chief Justice Marshall leaned in the opposite direction, and was so indiscreet as to dine with Burr at the home of John Wickham, chief counsel for the defense, while the proceeding was under way.

At one point, Marshall stated that he would subpoena Jefferson, directing him to bring to Richmond a certain document. The subpoena was served on the president, but a notation at the bottom stated that if he would furnish the court with the document, he would not have to come himself. Jefferson sent the paper. Thus the episode terminated without a showdown between Jefferson and Marshall over the right of the latter to command the president to appear.

After a trial lasting four months, the jury found that Burr was "not proved to be guilty" and hence was "not guilty." Jefferson was so angry over the outcome, and over various rulings Marshall had made as presiding judge, that he urged Marshall's impeachment. Nothing came of it.

For nearly three more decades Marshall sat on the Supreme Court. During those years he made his greatest contributions to the development of our system of constitutional law and to the building of the bone and sinew of the struggling republic.

An idea of the atmosphere in which the United States Supreme Court was operating can be found in the reaction of the Virginia Supreme Court in 1815 to the ruling of the highest court in *Martin v. Hunter's Lessee*. The state court unanimously refused to obey the order of the ranking court in the land. Yet the federal tribunal managed to get on record a vital opinion which fixed the pattern for the future relationship between our national and state courts.

Marshall's famous opinion a few years later in *McCulloch v. Maryland* upheld the supremacy of the national government against domination by the state governments. This opinion has been termed, in *Great American Lawyers*, edited by William Draper Lewis, "perhaps the most celebrated judicial utterance in the annals of the English-speaking world."

Other notable opinions rendered by Marshall during this period include those in *Cohens* v. *Virginia* and *Gibbons* v. *Ogden*.

In *Cohens* v. *Virginia* he held that Congress could lawfully pass an act permitting a citizen convicted in a state court to appeal to the United States Supreme Court, if he held that the state statute under which he was found guilty conflicted with the federal Constitution or an act of Congress. This case, together with *Marbury* v. *Madison*, established the Supreme Court as the final arbiter of the Constitution.

In *Gibbons* v. *Ogden*, Marshall greatly expanded the meaning of the term "commerce," as used in the nation's organic law. He ruled that the power of the Congress to regulate interstate and foreign commerce included not only the exchange of commodities but the means by which interstate and foreign commerce was carried on. He drew the conclusion that Congress had the right to license vessels to carry goods and passengers between states. Thus Marshall outlined the course which Congress was to follow in regulating interstate commerce.

These and other opinions by the Chief Justice protected the federal government from sabotage by the states, upheld the sanctity of contracts, safeguarded the material prosperity of the country, and ruled that business which was national in scope should be under national jurisdiction.

The dedicated state-righters, led by Thomas Jefferson, were sincerely alarmed by these decisions, for they believed Marshall to be imbued with "monarchical" and "aristocratical" ideas, and they feared the states would be virtually wiped out if the trend he represented continued. Despite the brilliance with which they themselves had contributed many essential concepts to the building of the republic, the Jeffersonians failed to grasp the absolute necessity for judicial action which would keep the weak and struggling nation from breaking apart. Consequently, they not only threatened to impeach the Chief Justice but they also tried to abolish the Supreme Court or reduce its power.

None of these attempts came to anything, and John Marshall continued on his course. But as his fame grew, he never lost his sense of humor. On one occasion a young attorney sought to flatter him by saying to him that he had reached "the acme of judicial distinction."

"Let me tell you what that means, young man," said the Chief Justice. "The acme of judicial distinction means the ability to look a lawyer straight in the eyes for two hours and not hear a damned word he says."

At one period, the Supreme Court adopted a rule that its members would take wine at meals only in wet weather. However, Justice Joseph Story wrote his wife:

"What I say about the wine gives you our rule; but it does sometimes happen that the Chief Justice will say to me, when the cloth is removed, 'Brother Story, step to the window and see if it does not look like rain.' And if I tell him that the sun is shining brightly, Judge Marshall will sometimes reply, 'All the better, for our jurisdiction extends over so large a territory that the doctrine of chances makes it certain that it must be raining somewhere.'"

Although John Marshall gave the Supreme Court immensely more prestige and authority than it had previously enjoyed, he approached the end of his life profoundly depressed over the trend of events. One reason was that the court was successfully defied by the state of Georgia in 1832, after the nation's top tribunal ordered the decision of the Georgia Supreme Court reversed in a case involving the Cherokee Indians. Georgia had brutally seized the lands of the Cherokees and annulled all their "laws, usages, and customs." The finding of the United States Supreme Court that these acts were illegal infuriated not only the Georgians but President Andrew Jackson. The latter reportedly challenged the Chief Justice with the words: "John Marshall has made his decision—now let him enforce it!" No enforcement was possible, and the mandate of the court was ignored.

This greatly disturbed Marshall, as did the fact that a majority of the court was tending to stray from the Federalist principles that he had championed. The first rumbling of the nullificationist movement in South Carolina and the mounting controversy over slavery also alarmed him. He feared for the permanence of the Union.

At about this time, too, his wife died, and his few remaining years were clouded with grief. "I have lost her, and with her have lost the solace of my life," he wrote in despair.

His own health began to fail, and he had to have an operation and painful medical treatments. He was heartened for a time by the ringing Nullification Proclamation, which, surprisingly, was issued by his old enemy, Andrew Jackson, informing the fiery South Carolinians that defiance of the national laws would be put down by force of arms. But nothing could permanently relieve his despondency, although he continued to do his work on the court almost until the very end. In the summer of 1835 his health declined further, and he went to Philadelphia for treatment. He died there on July 6, aged seventy-nine.

Two days before his death he had written the inscription for his tombstone, which merely gave the names of his parents, his wife, and himself, with the customary dates. He did not mention any of the exalted positions he had held.

The death of John Marshall brought an almost unprecedented outpouring of nationwide grief. Throughout the land there was mourning for the tall soldier of the Revolution and builder of the nation whose human traits caused him to be so widely loved, and whose flashing genius and incorruptible integrity marked him as one of the supreme jurists in world history.

Fittingly enough, the Liberty Bell was tolled from the tower of Independence Hall in Philadelphia. The crack which we see today in that relic of 1776 opened, according to legend, when its solemn tones marked the passing of Chief Justice Marshall, a great judge and an even greater man.

The Jefferson Scandals
(1981)

Rumors that Thomas Jefferson not only fathered slave children on his house servant Sally Hemings, but permitted them to be sold at auction, go all the way back to the vicious political campaign for the presidency in 1800. Recently they were given new life by Fawn Brodie in Thomas Jefferson: An Intimate History *(1974), and, for reasons having much more to do with contemporary needs and attitudes than with genuine historical zeal for truth, they have been picked up and accepted as fact by various commentators, scholarly and otherwise. The following is an examination of the substance of such charges made against the author of the Declaration of Independence.*

A record of extraordinary concealment" is the phrase used by Fawn Brodie in her *Thomas Jefferson: An Intimate History* (page 23) to describe Jefferson's relations with Sally Hemings. If the relations that she alleges actually existed, the description is fully justified.

"A serious passion that brought Jefferson and the slave woman much private happiness over a period lasting thirty-eight years," Brodie continues (page 32). "It also brought suffering, shame and even political paralysis in regard to Jefferson's agitation for emancipation."

James T. Callender, the original source of these charges, is termed "a generally accurate reporter" by Brodie. Just what this remarkable statement is based on remains a mystery. John C. Miller, the Stanford University historian, describes Callender as "the most unscrupulous scandalmonger of the day . . . a journalist who stopped at nothing and stooped to anything . . . truth, if it stood in his way, was summarily mowed down."

From *The Jefferson Scandals: A Rebuttal* (New York: Dodd Mead and Co., 1981).

This wildly irresponsible pamphleteer disseminated pages of falsehoods concerning, first, such Federalists as George Washington and John Adams, and then, reversing his allegiance, such Republicans as Thomas Jefferson and James Madison. In Callender's words, Washington was "a scandalous hypocrite" who "authorized the robbery and ruin of his own army" in the Revolution for his own private gain, while Adams was "a British spy" and "one of the most egregious fools upon the continent." Of Madison Callender wrote that "he must have known all about Sally, and when he assisted in passing off the president [Jefferson] as a prodigy of virtue, he differed from the president himself precisely as much as the man that circulates a copper dollar differs from the man that forged it."

No one, not even Callender, contended that Jefferson maintained a liaison with any slave woman until well after his wife's death in 1782. He and Martha Wayles Skelton had been married for a decade when she died, not long after the birth of their sixth child. (Only two of the children grew to maturity.) Jefferson's devotion to her was profound, and slaves present around her deathbed reported—although this was never proved—that the grief-stricken husband promised her not to marry again. When Martha died, at age thirty-three, Jefferson fainted and kept to his room for three weeks.

He was thirty-nine at the time of his beloved wife's passing. A few weeks before, he had declined reelection to the Virginia legislature, saying that he wished to retire from public life. The squire of Monticello had served for thirteen years in one capacity or another, including governor of Virginia and member of the Continental Congress, in which latter capacity he had penned the Declaration of Independence. His decision to withdraw from public office did not turn out to be irrevocable, for he was persuaded to serve again in the Continental Congress. There, in 1784, he presented a measure that would have prevented the spread of slavery into any territory beyond the original thirteen states. It was defeated by a single vote, and, as he wrote later, "heaven was silent in that awful moment." Adoption of this epochal measure would almost certainly have made the Civil War impossible. It was one of many evidences of Jefferson's far-reaching vision and his hatred of human slavery. Three years later, in the Ordinance of 1787, chattel servitude was prohibited in the region northwest of the Ohio River.

Jefferson also was prevailed upon to serve with John Adams and Benjamin Franklin on the commission to negotiate peace, following the achievement of American independence in the Revolution. When this mission became unnecessary, he was named, with Adams and Franklin, to negotiate treaties of commerce. He sailed for France in 1784 with his eleven-year-old daughter Martha, usually known as Patsy, intending to remain for two years. The stay turned out to be for five and a half years. Father and daughter had been in Paris only a few months when the sad news came that another daughter, Lucy Elizabeth, aged two and a half, had died of whooping cough. Hence Jefferson's only child left in Virginia was Mary, known as Maria or Polly, and her father became increasingly determined to bring her to Paris, to be with him and her older sister.

However, it would be years before the journey to France could be arranged. Polly was nine when she finally arrived in 1787, accompanied by the fourteen-year-old slave girl Sally Hemings. Jefferson had asked for a more mature woman as Polly's companion and maid, but this had not been feasible. James Hemings, Sally's older brother, had traveled to Paris with the Jeffersons in 1784.

The presence of youthful Sally in the Parisian entourage seemed innocent enough, and apparently nobody at the time felt that it had any significance except the obvious one, that Sally was serving as Polly's companion. But Madison Hemings, a son born to Sally years later in Virginia, was to claim in 1873, long after both Sally and Jefferson were dead, that his mother became Jefferson's concubine and that she first became pregnant by her master in Paris. Mrs. Brodie has accepted this assertion as true. Its validity will be examined hereafter.

Jefferson was appointed minister to France in 1785, as successor to Franklin, and in that post he kept his finger on the course of events. The rumblings of the oncoming French revolution were ominous and alarming, although so great a friend of the masses as he could not fail to sympathize with them in their genuine grievances. Jefferson wrote of the "monstrous abuses under which people were ground to powder," and he was not exaggerating. In a letter to James Madison in 1787 he also declared that "the king's passion for drink was divesting him of all respect, the queen was detested, and an explosion of some sort is not impossible." Two years later the Bastille fell (July 14, 1789), a few months before the Jeffersons returned to America, and Louis XVI and Marie Antoinette were on the road that would lead them ultimately to the guillotine. Jefferson was revolted by the excesses of the revolution, but he understood its causes better than most and was far more sympathetic to it than many Americans.

He had been diverted in 1786 from such serious concerns by his infatuation with Maria Cosway, the talented and charming wife of Richard Cosway, the most eminent English miniaturist of his time. Not much love was lost between the Cosways; Maria had apparently been talked into the marriage by her mother. Her husband was variously described as a fop and coxcomb who had affairs with other women and perhaps men.

Twenty-five letters between Jefferson and Maria Cosway suddenly surfaced in the 1940s in the papers of Jefferson's grandson, Thomas Jefferson Randolph. Jefferson had preserved them carefully, whereas he had destroyed his correspondence with his wife and his mother. It is obvious, therefore, that he did not object to their becoming available to posterity. Randolph apparently concluded in the nineteenth century that the time had not come to make them public, so he turned them over to his attorney and executor, in whose files they were found. Randolph, of course, could have destroyed them, but did not. They form the basis for the book *My Head and My Heart* by Helen Duprey Bullock. Mrs. Brodie observes darkly that "most of the letters were kept hidden by Jefferson's heirs until the 1940s, . . ." implying some sort of conspiracy among a number of people, for which there is no evidence.

Maria and Jefferson met in Paris in the autumn of 1786, and the forty-three-year-old widower, whose wife had died four years before, was attracted at once to the lovely twenty-seven-year-old woman with the golden hair and violet eyes. She was not only easy to look upon but greatly gifted both as an artist and a musician. At age nineteen she had been elected to the Academy of Fine Arts in Florence in her native Italy. (She was the daughter of a well-to-do English couple living there.) In the five years preceding her visit to Paris, she had twenty-two paintings exhibited at London's Royal Academy. Maria played well on the harp and pianoforte, was also a composer, and had a fine singing voice. In addition she was an accomplished linguist. All of which could not fail to appeal to Jefferson, whose interests were quite similar. Malone says "there can be no doubt that he fell deeply in love during that golden September," and there appears to be no reason to question it. Whether there was "illicit love-making" no one knows. "If he as a widower ever engaged in it," says Malone, "this was the time." Jefferson saw a great deal of Maria during these weeks until, when strolling with her one day in the Petit Cours he tried to jump a fence and fell. His right wrist was dislocated, and the excruciatingly painful injury not only prevented him from seeing her for a time, but forced him to learn to write with his left hand.

When she and her husband returned to London, he laboriously wrote her the famous letter "My Head and My Heart." In this extraordinary document he set forth at great length his struggles in determining whether his head or his heart was to have supremacy as he contemplated their relationship. They corresponded intermittently thereafter, in words that, at times, would seem to imply a passionate love affair. However, given the romantic phraseology of that era, it appears that not too much importance should be attached to these seemingly torrid endearments—especially since by the time Maria returned alone to Paris for nearly four months the following year, there had been a mutual cooling of the inner fires. Such is the opinion of Dumas Malone, Merrill Peterson, Helen Bullock, Nathan Shachner, and Charles van Pelt. But Fawn Brodie feels otherwise and says, without any documentation, that Maria "must certainly have been wracked by fears of pregnancy." Brodie also interprets Maria's words "I cannot be useful to you" in her farewell note to Jefferson before departing for London as meaning that perhaps "there had been some kind of crucial failure in the act of love." As with the reference to fears of pregnancy, this can only be pure supposition. There is no evidence that their relationship at that point involved fears of pregnancy or acts of love. On the contrary, there is reason to believe that if these things occurred, it was in the previous year.

They never saw each other again. Maria urged Jefferson in 1789 to stop over in London en route back to the United States, but he did not do so. He suggested that she visit America but seemed to discourage her from making the journey. Their subsequent correspondence was spasmodic. For example, in 1795 two letters arrived from Maria, who by that time had abandoned her husband. Jefferson did not reply for more than six months. Letters from her in 1823 and 1825, not long before his death, went unanswered.

Maria had always been religiously inclined, and her later correspondence with Jefferson was from a convent school for girls she had opened at Lodi, Italy. She spent the remainder of her days there and died in 1838. "In Milan and Lodi her death was regarded as a public calamity," Helen Bullock wrote in *My Head and My Heart*, "and her funeral was attended by members of the imperial family, by the dukes of all the neighboring municipalities, and by many of the religious orders."

Why did Jefferson's affair with Maria cool off so abruptly after it had begun so warmly in 1786? No one can say with certainty. Such a cooling happens to many lovers, for a variety of reasons. Mrs. Brodie is positive as to the explanation, namely that Jefferson began at this time his clandestine relationship with Sally and pretty well lost interest in Maria Cosway. "The evidence that the real rival was the comely little slave from Monticello, and that their affection began to bloom early in 1788, is complicated and subtle," she writes. Indeed it is; the real question is whether this "affection" ever existed.

Mrs. Brodie relies heavily on the statement given in 1873 by Madison Hemings, Sally's son, then living at Pee Pee, Pike County, Ohio, to the *Pike County Republican*. On its face, this declaration would seem to be convincing. The pertinent section follows:

> Their stay [in Paris] (my mother and Maria's) was about eighteen months. But during that time my mother became Mr. Jefferson's con-

cubine, and when he was called home she was *enciente* [*sic*] by him. He desired to bring my mother back to Virginia with him but she demurred. She was just beginning to understand the French language well, and in France she was free, while if she returned to Virginia she would be re-enslaved. So she refused to return with him. To induce her to do so he promised her extraordinary privileges, and made a solemn pledge that her children would be freed at the age of twenty-one years. In consequence of his promises, on which she implicitly relied, she returned with him to Virginia. Soon after their arrival she gave birth to a child, of whom Thomas Jefferson was the father. It lived but a short time. She gave birth to four others, and Jefferson was the father of all of them.

A number of things about the foregoing arouse one's doubts and suspicions. In the first place, the entire interview, as published, is in language that a poorly educated ex-slave would almost certainly not have used. Mrs. Brodie says Madison Hemings's reminiscences in the *Pike County Republican* are "most competently related," though possibly "corrected by the editor who printed them." It is more than a possibility that they were corrected; it is a virtual certainty. Consider the inclusion of the French word for "pregnant," *enceinte*—which, incidentally, was misspelled. Consider also the proficient use of English, more obvious in certain other passages than in the one quoted above. It sounds remarkably like the words of a newspaper editor or some other college-educated individual. Madison Hemings is quoted as saying, "I learned to read by inducing the white children to teach me the letters and something more; what else I know of books I have picked up here and there till now I can read and write." If all he learned was to read and write, where did that word *enceinte* come from, not to mention various other suspicious words and phrases?

There are also numerous inaccuracies. Since Hemings was an elderly man in 1873, talking about events that occurred before he was born in 1805, this is hardly surprising. But when Hemings states that Jefferson "had but little taste or care for agricultural pursuits," it is as absurd as if he had said that Jefferson was not interested in the construction of Monticello. The *Farm Book, Garden Book*, and dozens of letters and other documents attest to Jefferson's consuming interest in all things agricultural. Mrs. Brodie does not mention this and other misstatements, but accepts Madison's assertions concerning Jefferson's relationship with Sally as gospel. On this latter point, Madison must have been simply relating what his mother or someone else told him concerning his parentage.

Note that in discussing Sally's supposed concubinage in Paris, he declared that the child she bore "soon after their arrival [in the United States] . . . lived but a short time."

Mrs. Brodie ignores the foregoing assertion and declares that Sally gave birth soon after her return to a son named Tom who, she said, lived to be at least ten or twelve years old, and then disappeared mysteriously from Monticello. The first mention of this shadowy individual occurs in that authoritative journal the *Richmond Recorder* (September 1, 1802), edited by none other than James T. Callender. So we are indebted to Mrs. Brodie's "generally accurate reporter" for starting the crepuscular "Yellow Tom" on his mundane journey. Nobody has been able to nail him down or to prove that there was such a person. Brodie tries valiantly to trace Tom's movements after his supposed departure from Monticello. She mentions one tradition after another, admittedly uncertain as to whether any of them is correct. At one point she goes so far as to say, ". . . if he was, in truth, Jefferson and Sally Hemings's son . . ." We are left with the strong impression that Tom was just another figment of Callender's fertile imagination. John C. Miller of the Stanford history faculty writes, "Callender credited 'Tom,' whom he had never seen, with bearing a striking resemblance to the president. But no trace of the existence of 'Yellow Tom' has ever been discovered. . . . In actuality 'Yellow Tom' never existed." Winthrop D. Jordan agrees, as do Garry Wills, Merrill Peterson, and James Bear.

Understandably then, various careful students have concluded that Sally Hemings was not pregnant with Tom or anyone else when she returned from Paris in 1789. One of these was the late Douglass Adair, former editor of the prestigious *William and Mary Quarterly*, who made an exhaustive examination of the relevant evidence. His comprehensive findings are published in his posthumous work, *Fame and the Founding Fathers*.

With Malone, Boyd, and Peterson, Adair points to Jefferson's extremely complete *Farm Book* as one piece of important evidence. In it the master of Monticello kept a careful record of slave births on his mountaintop through three generations. In this volume the births of Sally Hemings and her children are meticulously set down. There is no record of any child being born to her soon after her arrival from Paris in 1789. If Jefferson recorded the other children he is supposed to have fathered, why would he have omitted the first? According to the *Farm Book*, Sally's first child was born in 1795.

Furthermore, in order for us to credit the story of Sally's having a baby soon after her arrival from France, we must believe that Jefferson, a conspicuously loving father by all the credible evidence, seduced a sixteen-year-old slave girl and traveled with her on shipboard, in an advanced state of pregnancy, in the intimate company of his two young daughters. Anyone familiar with his relationship with his children, testified to by scores of affectionate letters and every proof of adoration and concern, will find such a story altogether unbelievable.

We should bear in mind also that in 1873, when Madison Hemings and the editor of the *Pike County Republican* collaborated on their statement, the Civil War had ended only a short time before, and many Northerners were engaged in trying to make the slave-holding South of antebellum days seem as abhorrent as possible.

Madison Hemings not only contended in his interview that Jefferson had seduced Madison's mother in Paris; he likewise claimed that even after Callender had exposed this supposedly clandestine relationship in 1802, Thomas Jefferson, then president of the United States, was so utterly brazen and unconcerned for public opinion that he fathered two more children by her while still in the presidency.

Julian Boyd says that Hemings's statement "was obviously prompted by someone . . . shaped and perhaps even written and embellished by the prompter." And Dumas Malone, calling attention to the atmosphere of the time, assigns it a place "in the tradition of political enmity and abolitionist propaganda." The

Pike County Republican was edited by S. F. Wetmore, a native of Maine, who moved to Pike County after the Civil War and revived the local Republican paper. The rival Democratic journal was the *Waverly Watchman*. Both were published in the town of Waverly.

The *Waverly Watchman*, edited by John A. Jones, replied five days later (March 18, 1873) to the contentions attributed to Madison Hemings. Jones said, in part:

> We have no doubt but that there are at least fifty Negroes in this county who lay claim to illustrious parentage. . . . The children of Jefferson and Madison, Calhoun and Clay far outnumber Washington's body servants when Barnum was at the height of his prosperity. They are not to be blamed for making these assertions. It sounds much better for the mother to tell her offspring that 'master' is their father than to acknowledge to them that some field hand, without a name, had raised her to the dignity of a mother. . . . This is a well-known fact to those who have been reared in those states where slavery existed, and with them no attention whatever is paid to these rumors. . . . The fact that Hemings claims to be the natural son of Jefferson does not convince the world of its truthfulness.

Another reason why Sally may have told Madison that Jefferson was his father was that she wanted to protect the real father, who was a married man.

Near the end of 1873 (December 25) editor Wetmore returned to the attack in his paper. He had discovered another former Monticello slave, Israel Jefferson, who lived on Brushy Fork of Pee Pee Creek, Pebble Township. Israel submitted to an interview and was quoted as confirming Madison Hemings's claim that his mother was Thomas Jefferson's concubine, and that the author of the Declaration of Independence was the father of her children. "I can conscientiously confirm his [Madison's] statement as any other fact which I believe from circumstances but do not positively know," Israel is quoted as saying.

Mrs. Brodie concedes that "the reminiscences of Israel Jefferson . . . are written in so similar a style [to those of Madison Hemings] as to suggest that both memoirs were written by the same newspaperman after the interviews with these ex-slaves."

This is obvious when we note that Israel, like Madison, was able to do hardly more than read and write. Israel said in the aforementioned interview, "Since I have been in Ohio I have learned to read and write, but my duties as a laborer would not permit me to acquire much of an education." Yet consider the following example of his prose, as recorded by Wetmore:

Since my residence in Ohio I have several times visited Monticello. My last visit was in the fall of 1866. Near there I found the same [Thomas] Jefferson Randolph, whose service as administrator I left more than forty years ago, at Monticello. He had grown old, and was outwardly surrounded by the evidences of former ease and opulence gone to decay. He was in poverty. He had lost, he told me, $80,000 in money by joining the South in rebellion against the government. Except his real estate, the rebellion had stripped him of everything, save one blind mule. He said that if he had taken the advice of his sister, Mrs. Colleridge [Coolidge], gone to New York and remained there during the war, he could have saved the bulk of his property. But he was a rebel at heart, and chose to go with his people. Consequently, he was served as others had been—he had lost all his servants and nearly all his personal property of every kind. I went back to Virginia to find the proud and haughty Randolph in poverty, at Edge Hill, within four miles of Monticello, where he was bred and born. Indeed, I then realized more than ever before, the great changes which time brings about in the affairs and circumstances of life.

Like Madison Hemings, Israel Jefferson made a number of inaccurate statements. He said he had been born on Christmas Day, "the year I suppose was 1797," and "my earliest recollections are the exciting events surrounding the preparation of Mr. Jefferson and other members of his family on their removal to Washington" for his presidential inauguration. The *Farm Book* shows that Israel was born in 1800, not 1797. The Jeffersons moved to Washington in late 1800 or early 1801. Israel either hadn't been born or was a newly arrived baby. Hence his "recollections" are among the most precocious on record.

Israel also refers to Lafayette's visit to Monticello in 1824, saying that the Frenchman "remained with Mr. Jefferson six weeks, and almost every day I took them out to drive." Actually Lafayette was at Monticello only ten days.

So much for the contention of Israel Jefferson and Madison

Hemings that Thomas Jefferson was the father of Sally Hemings's children. It seems clear that their claims are subject to serious reservations and have many vulnerabilities.

In addition to the evidence that Mrs. Brodie finds in the words of James Callender and Madison Hemings to support her thesis that Jefferson had a thirty-eight-year relationship with Sally Hemings, there are her psychological interpretations. These are rejected out of hand by many historians, but they permeate her biography.

For example, Jefferson made a seven-week tour of several European countries in 1788 and kept a diary. "Anyone who reads with care these twenty-five pages must find it singular that in describing the countryside . . . he used the word 'mulatto' eight times," writes Mrs. Brodie. He was describing the color of the soil. On a tour in the previous year he had used the term "mulatto" only once, she says.

There are also her references to the shape of the plough and the women he saw in the fields. "Considering the ancient symbolism of the plough," writes Brodie, "it is not surprising, perhaps, that writing about the ideal shape of the ancient and basic agricultural tool led him immediately to observations about the women he had seen in the fields who followed close behind it." Mrs. Brodie does not elaborate upon the "ancient symbolism of the plough," and we are left in the dark as to just what the symbolism is. One is reminded of her cryptic reference (page 79) to the fig's "ancient symbolic history, relating to both love and sin," apropos of Jefferson's action in sending a basket of figs to the dying John Walker in 1809.

At all events, she quotes Jefferson as follows concerning the women he saw in the fields on his European tour:

> The women here . . . do all sorts of work. While one considers them as useful and rational companions, one cannot forget that they are also the objects of our pleasures. Nor can they ever forget it. While employed in dirt and drudgery some tag of ribbon, some ring or bit of bracelet, earbob or necklace, or something of that kind will shew that the desire of pleasing is never suspended in them . . . They are formed by nature for attentions and not for hard labor.

Mrs. Brodie concludes from the foregoing: "This is all very tender and suggests that he was thinking not at all about the splendidly dressed Maria Cosway when he wrote it."

Equally far-fetched is Brodie's interpretation of Jefferson's letter to Maria upon his return to Paris: "He described briefly his return to Germany, with a glowing description of the art gallery at Düsseldorf. Here, in describing the painting that excited him above all others, he betrayed, inadvertently as a man often does to an old love, that he had been captured by a new one." The extract from his letter follows:

> At Dusseldorp I wished for you much. I surely never saw so precious a collection of paintings. Above all things those of Van der Werff affected me the most. His picture of Sarah delivering Agar to Abraham is delicious. I would have agreed to have been Abraham though the consequences would have been that I should have been dead five or six thousand years. . . . I am but a son of nature, loving what I see and feel, without being able to give a reason, nor caring much whether there be one.

Mrs. Brodie then affords us the following insight into Jefferson's true meaning:

> "Agar"—Hagar the Egyptian—it will be remembered was Abraham's concubine, given to him by his wife Sarah when she could not bear a child, and destined to become the legendary mother of the Arab peoples. In this painting she is pictured as very young, partly nude, but seductive in a fashion that is innocence itself. She is blond, with long straight hair down her back. Abraham, though bearded, is far from old, with the nude shoulders and chest of a young and vigorous giant . . .
>
> Although Jefferson included tender passages in this letter to Maria Cosway . . . he confessed callously that he had found it impossible to write a letter to her on the whole seven-week journey. "At Strasbourg I sat down to write you," he admitted. "But for my soul I could think of nothing at Strasbourg but the promontory of noses, of Diego, of Slawkenburgius the historian, and the procession of Strasburgers to meet the man with the nose. . . ."

"Maria Cosway was not only baffled but enraged," writes Brodie. "'How could you led me by the hand all the way [Cosway, as a native of Italy, wrote awkward English] think of me, have

Many things to say, and not find One word to write *but on Noses?*'"

And Brodie provides us with the following truly extraordinary interpretation:

> One may well echo Maria Cosway's question, "Why noses?" As we have already asked, "Why mulatto?" Jefferson's bemusement with the one may well have been related to the other. If Sally Hemings, though "mighty near white," retained a suggestion of her grandmother's physical heritage in the shape of her nose, it could be that Jefferson, caught up in a new passion, was cursing the world's insistence on caring about such matters. Though his preoccupation with this girl of mixed blood did not cost him a city, as did the preoccupation of the Strasbourgers with a nose, it would eventually threaten to cost him the presidency.

Mrs. Brodie mentions all this as though it had some profound significance, a significance that will, we daresay, escape most readers. Furthermore, she refers to an imaginary "threat to his presidency." Evidence of this "threat" is hard to find; indeed it appears to be nonexistent. Malone says Jefferson's "political position had never seemed more secure than in the autumn of 1804 [two years following Callender's "revelations"], for it was then that he was triumphantly reelected"—in a landslide.

We come next to Brodie's discovery that in mentioning an orangutan in a letter to Maria Cosway, Jefferson inadvertently let the monkey out of the bag with respect to Sally Hemings. January 1789 was one of the coldest Januaries on record in Paris, for carriages were crossing the Seine on the ice. "Surely it was never so cold before," Jefferson wrote. "To me who am an animal of a warm climate, a mere Oran-ootan, it has been a severe trial." Mrs. Brodie comments:

> We do not know exactly what Jefferson conceived an "Oran-ootan" to be but we do know that in his *Notes on the State of Virginia*, published only a few months before Sally Hemings's arrival, he had indiscreetly written that blacks preferred whites over their own species, just as the "Oran-ootan" preferred "the black woman over those of his own species." That he may now suddenly have become uneasy about what he had written concerning this mysterious man of nature, or man of the woods, is suggested by the fact that on Oct. 2, 1788, when he sent

away to his London bookdealer for a list of books for purchase, he included E. Tyson's *Oran-outang: or, An Anatomy of a Pigmy* (1699). . . . Jefferson had good reason to be uncomfortable. For when the Federalist press in America later heard rumors about his slave paramour, the editors needled him cruelly on this very passage in his *Notes*.

Just what all this proves may have been clear to Mrs. Brodie, but it leaves many others baffled.

She writes (page 233) that "there is also what one might call hard evidence that Jefferson in Paris treated Sally Hemings with special consideration." It seems that he paid 240 francs for a smallpox inoculation for Sally, "a very great sum." So it was, but if Jefferson didn't want an outbreak of the disease in his entourage, what alternative did he have? James Bear says the figure "most probably included room and board for the six weeks or more period of quarantine." Mrs. Brodie mentions that a French tutor was engaged for Sally, apparently Monsieur Perrault, who was also tutoring James. The latter was evidently a trial for the gentleman, who sought on one occasion to collect for his services during the preceding twenty months only to be punched and kicked by James, who tore Perrault's only overcoat. Small wonder that the tutor, in remonstrating to Jefferson, complained of "*sottises les plus dures*" ("most frightful stupidities"). No doubt Jefferson saw that the bill was paid. As for wages, James and Sally were on an equal footing—each was paid 24 francs a month, beginning in 1788. Brodie tells us that in 1789 Jefferson suddenly began spending "a surprising amount of money on Sally's clothes." However, the outlays for Patsy's clothes were "several times" as much. Since Jefferson, as United States minister, was moving in the highest circles of France, it is hardly to be expected that his daughter's companion would under any circumstances have been shoddily dressed. The record as to these expenditures "seems to have been kept as secret as possible," says Brodie, without offering any evidence.

And there are those missing letters of Jefferson's for "this critical year of 1788 . . . the only volume missing in the whole forty-three-year epistolary record. " Among the communications that disappeared were letters that he wrote his daughters. "This raises the question whether or not someone at some time went through Jefferson's papers systematically eliminating every possible reference to Sally Hemings," writes the ever-suspicious Mrs. Brodie. (Why, then, were the daughters' letters also "eliminated"?) Letters from Jefferson to Sally's brothers and from her brothers to him are extant. But no letters or notes exchanged between Sally Hemings and Thomas Jefferson have as yet found their way into the public record. One explanation could be that there never were any. As David Herbert Donald, the Pulitzer Prize–winning Harvard historian, wrote in reviewing Brodie's Jefferson biography for *Commentary*: "Mrs. Brodie is masterful in using negative evidence. . . . The fact that Jefferson's *Farm Book*, in which he scrupulously itemized all his expenses, shows that he gave no favorite treatment to Sally and her offspring can only mean that he was surreptitiously slipping her the money that he listed under 'Charity.'"

A new situation presents itself, Donald points out, "when there is no evidence whatever to cloud her [Brodie's] vision," for then "she is free to speculate."

"It seems likely . . . One can only guess . . ." she begins a paragraph describing Sally's feelings upon returning from France to America and to slavery. "No one can know," she says of Jefferson's sentiments on this occasion—and then proceeds to reveal in detail what he must have felt. Where there are no troublesome documents, Mrs. Brodie can offer proof by coincidence: is it not significant that Jefferson's daughter decided to become a nun during the same month that he ordered some clothing for his slave Sally? And is it not even more revealing that another Jefferson daughter married and left home shortly after Sally gave birth to one of her numerous children? In the absence of any reference to Sally in all the letters of Jefferson and his daughters, does not silence constitute overwhelming evidence that the daughters knew all about the affair with the slave girl and disapproved of it?

We continue with examples of Mrs. Brodie's psychological approach to the doings of the wayward Mr. Jefferson.

During the latter's affair with Mrs. Cosway in Paris, John Trumbull, the portrait painter, wrote him from London that Mrs. Cosway's husband and various of her friends were annoyed that they had not received a single line from her in three weeks. Jefferson replied, in part, to Trumbull, "So many infidelities in the postoffice are complained of since the rumors of war have arisen that I have waited a safer opportunity of enclosing you a bill of exchange." Mrs. Brodie comments, "Here, it would seem, he came very close to saying what was really bothering him—*so many complaints of our infidelities are coming through the postoffice.*"

Upon returning to Monticello in 1794 from service in Washington's cabinet, Jefferson wrote several letters expressing his intense pleasure at once more experiencing the joys of rural life. To a French friend he declared, "I have returned with infinite appetite to the enjoyment of my farm, my family and my books." To John Adams he wrote, "I return to farming with an ardor that I scarcely knew in my youth," and to James Madison, "I find my mind totally absorbed in my rural occupations." Mrs. Brodie, with Sally Hemings on her mind, comes up with the following exegesis: "Infinitely the happier, totally absorbed, ardor, infinite appetite—these are strong words, with the unmistakable flavor of sexuality. They suggest that satisfactions of the body at Monticello were real." Which led David Donald to observe in his review that Brodie "appears to be a disciple of the late A. C. Kinsey and believes that a man should be judged by the fullness and frequency of his sex life." He adds: "She ought to have given her book a better title. Why not 'By Sex Obsessed'?" Pursuing this theme further, Donald observes, apropos of her interpretation of Jefferson's reference in his John Trumbull letter to "infidelities of the postoffice," "One presumes that when Jefferson wrote Ralph Izard about 'infidelities of the postoffice' he was giving a hint of homosexual passion that Mrs. Brodie had inexcusably overlooked."

A parenthetical reference in Jefferson's famous letter to James Madison from Paris in 1789, in which Jefferson enunciated his view that "the earth belongs in usufruct to the living" is interpreted by Mrs. Brodie as signifying that Jefferson was thinking of Sally Hemings. His experience as minister to France "destroyed any lingering puritanical legacy from his childhood," she says, "broadened his compassion for anyone caught up in the delights and difficulties of extramarital adventure, and confirmed his private conviction that a man is master of his own body and may govern it as he pleases." In considering this lengthy communication, covering several pages and devoted to serious discussion of "political relativism" and the question whether "one generation of men has a right to bind another," with special emphasis on "the power of contracting debts," Mrs. Brodie focuses on a single brief sentence. Jefferson wrote Madison from Paris, in part, as follows: "The earth belongs always to the living generation. They may manage it, then, and what proceeds from it, as they please, during their usufruct. *They are masters, too, of their own persons, and consequently may govern them as they please* [italics supplied]. But persons and property make the sum of the objects of government. The institutions and laws of their predecessors extinguished them in their natural course with those who gave them being. . . ." Mrs. Brodie leaps upon the foregoing italicized statement and provides this comment (pages 244–245): "Almost none of this was obvious in his own time, and is evident today only if one scrutinizes letters which Jefferson's heirs for many years took pains to hide. Here if anywhere one finds the answer to the question whether Jefferson embraced the monastic and continent life ascribed to him by so many, or whether his vital sexuality, instead of atrophying, reasserted itself to make possible a new, if hidden happiness."

To support the foregoing sweeping assertion, Mrs. Brodie provides no evidence at all, except a footnote calling attention to Jefferson's above-quoted letter to Madison. In her reiterated reference to "letters which Jefferson's heirs for many years took pains to hide," she apparently has in mind the letters between Jefferson and Maria Cosway, in which Sally Hemings is nowhere mentioned, and which seem temporarily to have been pigeonholed by Jefferson's grandson; and the letter from Ellen Coolidge, his granddaughter, to her husband, which was not released for publication in its entirety until 1974. This latter communication, far from supporting Mrs. Brodie's contentions as to Jefferson's supposed miscegenation, provides some of the most striking evidence as to their incorrectness. Upon such gauzy foundations, Mrs. Brodie erects far-reaching conclusions as to the reassertion by Jefferson of his "vital sexuality."

A still more extraordinary interpretation comes to us on page 284 of her Jefferson biography. Edwin M. Yoder, Jr., commenting in *National Review* (May 10, 1974) on this passage, makes the following observation: "Of all these strained speculations, the prize must surely be given to her suggestion that when Jefferson decided to remodel Monticello after his sojourn in France, 'the possibility can be suggested that since buildings often symbolize in dreams the body of a woman, Jefferson . . . may have been unconsciously defining and redefining his ideal woman.'" Yoder goes on to say, "It can be suggested also that Jefferson, who tinkered with his house and grounds constantly for some forty years, wanted to incorporate the new architectural ideas he had garnered in Europe."

There is also Brodie's interpretation of Jefferson's *Syllabus of an Estimate of the Doctrine of Jesus*, which she says is "generally described simply as a defense against the continuing public libel that he was an atheist," but is actually "much more an attempt at a resolution of a shattering personal dilemma." She goes on to state that "his affection for Sally Hemings, and hers for him, long a private and inoffensive secret, had been turned into political pornography." Mrs. Brodie then says, "So Jefferson began his syllabus with a curious sentence: 'In a comparative view of the Ethics of the enlightened nations of antiquity, of the Jews and of Jesus, no notice should be taken of the corruptions of reason among the ancients, to wit, the idolatry and superstition of the vulgar, nor the corruptions of Christianity by the learned among its professors.'" The fact that there is anything "curious" about the foregoing sentence had indeed escaped the attention of the leading students of Jefferson's thought processes and religious beliefs. Unfortunately these students were males, and hence not equipped with the "feeling" and "nuance" which, according to Mrs. Brodie, are vouchsafed only to women—males, it appears, are incapable of understanding "Jefferson and the life of the heart." So she provides us with the true explanation. "Could the repetition of the word 'corruption' suggest that he was not so much contemplating the 'corruptions of Christianity' or the 'corruptions of reason' as the corruptions of Thomas Jefferson?" she asks. "That he was defensive and anxious shows not only in the document itself but also in the letters accompanying it, which he sent to his daughters and Benjamin Rush." He wrote Martha that he was placing "my religious creed on paper," and that he wished his family to have the syllabus, so that they might be able to "estimate the libels published against me on this, as on every possible other subject." Jefferson wrote Benjamin Rush in a similar vein, saying that he felt no obligation to any "inquisition over the rights of conscience," since questions of faith were a private matter "between God and himself." Brodie adds, incomprehensibly, "So, too, he seems to have been saying, were questions of the heart."

On such foundations she has erected her case for the grave charges she has brought against Thomas Jefferson.

Life at the Early University
(1981)

The university finally opened its doors in March 1825 after various delays. The entering class numbered only about 40 students, a figure that would rise to 116 by the end of the year—far fewer than had been expected. Efforts to obtain several distinguished Americans for the faculty had failed, and Francis Walker Gilmer, a young native of Albemarle whom Jefferson had termed "the best-educated subject we have raised since the Revolution," had been sent to England and Scotland to round up a teaching staff. He managed to engage five talented young men and get them across the ocean in time for classes to begin.

They were George Long, who would occupy the chair of ancient languages, and Thomas H. Key, mathematics, both from Cambridge University; Robley Dunglison, with a wide reputation as a writer on medical subjects, who would instruct in medicine; Charles Bonnycastle, son of a noted mathematician, to occupy the chair of natural philosophy; and George Blaettermann, a German living in England, modern languages. John P. Emmet, a native of Ireland and nephew of the famous Irish patriot Robert Emmet, was brought from Charleston, S.C., to give courses in natural philosophy.

Dr. Robley Dunglison was "the first full-time professor of medicine in an American university," and a novel feature of his contract, unheard of at the time in America, was the restriction of his practice outside the university to consultation, Dr. Wilhelm Moll, director of the university's health sciences laboratory, wrote

From *Mr. Jefferson's University: A History* (Charlottesville: University Press of Virginia, 1981).

in the *Virginia Medical Monthly*. Another innovation under Dunglison was his decision to issue medical diplomas in English rather than Latin so that they "may be intelligible to everyone."

Seven of the eight chairs had been filled when the university opened in 1825, only that of law being vacant. It was felt that law and moral philosophy, or ethics, ought to be taught by Americans. The brilliant and versatile William Wirt, then attorney general of the United States and chief prosecutor of Aaron Burr at his trial for treason in 1807, was offered the professorship of law, along with the presidency of the university. Jefferson had not contemplated electing anyone president of the institution, since he preferred a chairman of the faculty, but in order to get Wirt it was felt necessary to offer him the two positions. He declined, and the university continued to operate for the rest of the century with a rotating chairman of the faculty. During that period it was the only college or university of stature in the United States that functioned under this system.

When Wirt was found to be unavailable, John T. Lomax, a well-known Fredericksburg attorney, was chosen professor of law. The chair of moral philosophy was tendered to George Tucker, member of Congress and distinguished author in the field of both fiction and finance. Tucker, decidedly the eldest, was named the first chairman.

It has frequently been stated that Jefferson was unwilling to allow the law students even to study the doctrines of the hated Federalists and that no textbooks setting forth those doctrines were allowed. Such was, indeed, Jefferson's desire, but at the instigation of Madison the plan was modified for the better. The *Federalist Papers* were accordingly included. Also there was no restriction on the use of additional books.

Jefferson invited all the students in the university to dine with him in small groups on his mountaintop. One who entered about a year after the institution opened, and remained only about ten months, was Edgar Allan Poe, who is presumed to have sat at Jefferson's table. Poe's record as a student is by no means as lurid as is commonly supposed. Although he incurred heavy gambling debts, in part because his foster father, John Allan, refused to furnish him with enough funds to meet his minimum expenses, the amount of his drinking, then and later, is authoritatively stated to have been exaggerated. He made an excellent scholastic record at the university and was not in trouble at any time with the authorities, in contrast to the riotous behavior of many others enrolled there.

Jefferson had worked out a plan for student self-government, for he believed that young men from the best families could be counted on to govern themselves and remain reasonably well-behaved. He was promptly disillusioned. It was an age when youth was in rebellion against authority, in both North and South. Riots on college campuses were frequent, and the institution at Charlottesville was no exception.

Many of the young men there apparently had been accustomed at home to carrying firearms and to drinking and gambling. Given almost complete freedom at the university, they soon became disorderly. Several times during that first summer there were "vicious irregularities," as Jefferson phrased it, and then in the early autumn almost unbelievable rowdyism erupted.

"Down with the European professors!" was the cry of a crowd of masked students gathered on the Lawn after dark. Professors Emmet and Tucker went to investigate the uproar. Emmet seized hold of a counterpane in which one student had wrapped himself, whereupon another student threw a brick at him. Tucker was attacked with a cane, and vulgar abuse was hurled at the two professors amid loud and derisive howls. As if this were not enough, sixty-five students signed a resolution next day sharply assailing Emmet and Tucker for daring to lay hands upon the bedraped student! Not surprisingly, the faculty announced that if effective policing were not put into effect at once, they would all resign.

On Jefferson's recommendation, the Board of Visitors accordingly adopted extremely strict regulations, and the students most seriously involved in the riot were expelled. The visitors ordered every student to retire to his room at 9 o'clock each night and to arise with the dawn and eat breakfast by candlelight. All had to wear an officially prescribed dull gray uniform. Gambling, smoking, and drinking were forbidden, and students were required to deposit all their funds with the proctor, who could dole out small sums according to his whims.

These draconian rules were deeply resented, but things remained relatively quiet until 1831, when another riot occurred. Then in 1836 still worse disorder broke out. Many windows in the pavilions were smashed with stones and sticks, there was much firing of muskets under the arcades, and the uneasy professors armed themselves and fled with their families to the upper floors. Two years later, in another outburst, the pavilion of Prof. William Barton Rogers was attacked, many windows were broken, and the door was battered down. The following year Prof. Gessner Harrison, chairman of the faculty, was assaulted by two students and horsewhipped while at least one hundred other students looked on and did nothing to stop the outrage.

But the climactic atrocity occurred in 1840. Two students were firing shots and making an uproar on the Lawn, and John A. G. Davis, chairman of the faculty and professor of law, came out of his residence in Pavilion X to investigate. One of the students was masked; Davis approached him and tried to remove the mask in order to identify him. The youth, Joseph E. Semmes of Georgia, drew a pistol and shot Davis, wounding him fatally. Semmes was apprehended, and while awaiting trial was released on $25,000 bail. He disappeared and is said to have committed suicide.

The murder of the faculty's admired chairman sent shock waves throughout the state and beyond. It had the effect of bringing university students at least temporarily to their senses, and while there were other disorders, the number of such episodes tended to diminish with the years. Moreover, the Honor System was introduced in 1842, and its success was in part due to the new and more serious mood.

Henry St. George Tucker, a distinguished judge, was appointed professor of law to succeed the slain Davis. Judge Tucker soon became aware of the rankling resentment engendered by the uniform and early rising regulations, which were still in effect. He took a leading role in obtaining revocation of the obnoxious rules. He also noted the atmosphere of suspicion surrounding examinations, during which faculty members watched the young men closely to prevent cheating. Tucker accordingly recommended that each student be required to sign a statement that he had received no assistance. This was done, and the declaration was expanded later to include a pledge that no assistance had been given to anyone else. Members of the faculty continued to keep watch in the examination room, but this surveillance was lifted gradually. After the Civil War the Honor System as it is known today came into being, with students in full control and without faculty supervision or participation.

At both ends of the two Ranges, and in the middle of each, was a structure called a "hotel," larger than the adjacent rooms for students. In these buildings, which are used today for other purposes, the students had their meals. During the first half-dozen years after the university opened, the food is said to have been satisfactory, but then came fervent complaints that the menus were lacking in variety and the cooking execrable. The boys vented their ire by throwing rolls at each other in the dining room and engaging in other forms of disorder. The hotelkeepers, for their part, stated that their charge for the meals, fixed by the university, was so low that they could not afford any better fare. In 1849 the General Assembly decreed that meals for the students should be free of charge and paid for by the state, but this legislation was repealed seven years later.

Although the university had been founded on the principle of complete separation of church and state, it was not intended that all religion be discouraged. On the contrary, Jefferson set aside a room in the Rotunda for religious services, and in 1832 the students initiated a movement, with approval of the faculty and visitors, to raise funds for the employment of a chaplain. Within two years the effort was successful, and the chaplaincy was made permanent. The occupant of the post was elected annually by the faculty, with Episcopalians, Presbyterians, Methodists, and Baptists furnishing the chaplain in rotation. While it was deemed improper for him to have an official connection with the institution (his salary was paid with private funds), the above-mentioned room in the Rotunda was used by him as a chapel. In 1855 a parsonage was erected below the south end of the Lawn.

No clergyman was employed on the university faculty in the early years, for Thomas Jefferson was firmly opposed to any such direct denominational relationship. It was not until the Reverend William Holmes McGuffey, a Presbyterian, joined the teaching staff in 1845 as professor of moral philosophy that this principle was breached. The presence on the faculty of "Old Guff," as he was called by the students, tended to counteract the impression that the university was an "infidel institution."

A professor, in the beginning, received a free residence in one of the Lawn pavilions and a salary of $1,500, plus a $25 fee for each of his students. Some classes were large, and those teachers enjoyed substantial incomes from fees, while others with smaller classes were not so well situated. This caused unhappiness, and in 1850 the fee system was finally abandoned in favor of a flat annual salary of $3,000 for all.

There were other problems with the professors, in addition to those involving compensation. For example, the German-born Blaettermann was arbitrary, temperamental, and apparently endowed with a Prussian personality. He engaged in heated altercations with his students, and his lectures were interrupted by loud noises emanating from various parts of the classroom. On one occasion, Blaettermann knocked a student's hat off, and the latter punched the professor repeatedly. Blaettermann's relations with his wife were equally hectic and unconventional, for he was given to cowhiding her both in private and in public. Blaettermann was finally dismissed by unanimous vote of the Visitors.

His place was filled by Charles Kraitsir, a Hungarian, who, like Blaettermann, was a wizard with modern languages. But Kraitsir's lectures were unpopular, his fees fell off in consequence, and he was unhappy; at the same time, his colleagues on the faculty were disappointed with his performance as a teacher. On top of all else, his wife, a powerful woman, was in the habit of beating him and turning him out of the house in the middle of the night.

Kraitsir was dropped from the faculty. He complained: "The Board of Visitors . . . was hard to please. They kicked Dr. Blaettermann out because he whipped his wife, and they kicked me out because I have been whipped by my wife. What did they really want?"

In the early days of the university's history, about two-thirds of the students were dropped at the end of their first year for failure to meet scholastic requirements or for flagrant violations of the regulations. Approximately as many were usually eliminated after the first session in years immediately following the Civil War.

The boys rightly resented the early-rising rules, which remained in effect for nearly two decades, but disregard of these requirements was less frequent than might be imagined. And it is hardly surprising that the student's rooms along the Lawn and Ranges were often in a disordered state, that the simple furniture was knocked about, or that tobacco juice stained the walls at times.

A black slave, hired by the hotelkeeper responsible for each group of rooms, entered the apartment at about 6 A.M. daily, bearing a pitcher of water, often at near-freezing temperatures. He started the fire in the grate and cleaned the shoes. After the student had dressed in great haste and hurried to breakfast by candlelight in the nearby hotel, the slave made up the beds, swept the floor, and carried out the ashes. In winter he brought wood for the fireplace and in summer ice. Candles were the only form of illumination in the rooms and elsewhere until about 1838, when oil lamps came into vogue.

The dress of the students in those far-off days was astonishing by modern standards. Frock or swallowtail coats were the prevailing mode, while "the more daring wore their calico study gowns to lecture as well as to meals," said Frederick W. Page, writing concerning the sartorial situation as of 1843.

Diversions were bucolic and uninspiring by today's criteria. Classes lasted from 7:30 A.M. to 4:30 P.M., which left little time for much else, especially since early-rising and in-the-room-by-9-P.M. requirements continued until the mid-1840s. An athletic instructor, with primitive facilities, taught boxing, fencing, and quarter-staff, or single stick. Instruction was given in two low structures with flat roofs adjoining the basement of the Rotunda on the east and west. Intercollegiate sports were, of course, unknown.

In the 1850s a Pole named J. E. D'Alfonce operated a gymnasium for the students in which he put them through various exercises on parallel bars, ladders, and ropes. Authority for construction of a new gymnasium, at the modest cost of $1,500, was granted in 1857 by the Board of Visitors. The edifice thus erected was termed by the student magazine "a mere apology for a gymnasium."

Walks in the country on Sunday, the only free day, provided one form of relaxation for the young men. Playing of musical instruments was indulged in, but this was forbidden during class hours and on Sunday. By special dispensation, the boys were allowed to go to Charlottesville on the Sabbath, where they could even attend parties. Neither horses nor dogs could be kept by the students, nor were cockfights allowed, but the last-named form of divertissement was sometimes engaged in surreptitiously. Pitching quoits and the game of marbles had numerous adherents, but quoits too was forbidden on Sunday. Skating in winter on the pond near the site of the present university chapel was enjoyed when the ice was sufficiently thick.

It should be emphasized that Bacchanalian revels were not the regular order of the day or night and that these occurred mainly on special occasions and at fairly wide intervals. In the 1850s those who were found to be transgressing heinously were given the alternative of signing the pledge with the Temperance Society or being expelled. Many chose the former option.

During the years when the obnoxious uniform and early-rising rules held sway, the boys couldn't even have "a little chicken supper" in their rooms without permission from the chairman of the faculty. But with the elimination of these restrictions, it became possible for students to have meals in their quarters, provided there was no liquor.

An amusing extracurricular feature was the annual ceremony

on the Lawn held by what was named the "Ugly Club." It involved selection of the "ugliest man" in the student body, as well as the "prettiest man" and the "vainest man." The "ugliest man" had to accept his prize of a $15 pair of boots with an appropriately humorous speech.

"Laughing-Gas Day" was another yearly event on the Lawn. The professor of chemistry provided the gas and administered it to a previously selected victim. The latter thereupon went into a series of extraordinary antics, laughing hysterically and otherwise making a spectacle of himself. In fact, one student was so overcome that he indulged in what was termed improper behavior, and Laughing-Gas Day was discontinued.

The "dyke" and the "calathump" were forms of student diversion during these years which continued into the era immediately following the war. The dyke was a concerted effort on the part of students to embarrass any fellow collegian who was found to be en route to a rendezvous with his fair one. On such occasions, all the noisemaking apparatus that could be assembled, such as drums, horns, whistles, and coal scuttles belabored with pokers, was brought into action. The shouting and screeching crowd surrounded the young man and accompanied him as far as his ladylove's door. If it was at night, the participants in the dyke carried improvised torches. Often the youth was required to make a few brief remarks to the assembled multitude before he was permitted to enter the home of his inamorata. At times the mob lay in wait until he emerged, whereupon it greeted him with raucous din and ear-splitting cacophony.

A calathump was another form of frolic in the mid-nineteenth century and after. It began innocently enough with the formation of a college band known as the Calathumpians, who serenaded the professors on the Lawn. But a disorderly element got control, and there was not only a great deal of noise but in 1845 the Calathumpians launched a prolonged disturbance during which they smashed blinds and windows on the professors' pavilions and even damaged the Rotunda. This particular riot was so violent that the university authorities called out the militia, which calmed the situation, at least temporarily.

The university's prestige was so impaired throughout Virginia and beyond by these disorders, and the earlier murder of Professor Davis, that a group of prominent alumni issued a statement designed to put the situation at the institution in perspective. They pointed to the training of innumerable young men by the university, men who had taken positions of leadership, and emphasized that it was not a place for educating just the sons of the rich since many students were having to work their way through. The alumni also protested the small size of the annual state appropriation to the institution, still only $15,000, and the low scale of professors' salaries. They noted that one of their group, while a student at Harvard, had witnessed an assault by his fellow collegians on a regiment of militia. Evidently such behavior was by no means limited to students at the University of Virginia.

Edgar Allan Poe in Richmond
(1976)

A familiar figure in Richmond from time to time during the 1820s, 1830s, and 1840s was Edgar Allan Poe. Upon the death of his mother in 1811 when he was less than three years old, Edgar was taken into the household of John Allan, a member of the mercantile firm of Ellis & Allan. The boy was given the middle name of Allan, although he was not related to the family.

Poe was "beautiful, yet brave and manly for one so young," and "a leader among his playmates," Thomas Ellis wrote many years later. Charles Ellis, partner of John Allan and father of Tom, said Poe was "trained in all the habits of the most polished society," and he added that "there was not a brighter, more graceful or more attractive boy in the city." Young Edgar attended Monumental Episcopal Church with his foster parents.

Frustration, poverty, and near-starvation in later years changed Poe's personality. His break with John Allan in the mid-1820s contributed to this dramatic metamorphosis. He once termed "the want of parental affection . . . the heaviest of my trials."

When the orphaned boy joined the household of the childless Allans, they were living over the Ellis & Allan store at the northeast corner of Thirteenth and Main. It was not unusual in Richmond at the time to live over one's store, although the well-to-do merchants had their commodious residences, complete with garden, stable, and other dependencies. The Allans went to England in 1816 and remained five years, taking Edgar with them. The

From *Richmond: The Story of a City* (Garden City, N.Y.: Doubleday and Co., 1976).

boy was there from ages six to eleven. Allan was interested in opening an English branch of his firm.

Upon the return of the Allans, they lived for nearly a year in the home of Charles Ellis, on the southwest corner of Second and Franklin. Poe played as a boy in Ellis's "enchanted garden." The garden, with its jasmine and roses, its myrtle and honeysuckle, its flowering shrubs and twittering birds, was across Franklin on the site of the eastern half of today's Linden Row. The linden trees which lined the block gave their name to Linden Square and to the handsome row of ten Greek Revival houses built there in the mid-nineteenth century.

On leaving the Ellis home, the Allans took a "long low cottage house on Fifth Street, fronting west, between Marshall and Clay Streets." They moved thence to a house at the northwest corner of Fourteenth Street and Tobacco Alley, and were there in 1825 when Allan's uncle, William Galt, a prominent Richmond merchant, died and left him a fortune.

Allan promptly purchased the handsome house, Moldavia, at the southeast corner of Fifth and Main. It had been bought from the David Meade Randolphs by Joseph Gallego, the wealthy miller, who lived there until his death in 1818. Gallego never recovered from his wife's death in the devastating theater fire of 1811.

Poe was now sixteen and preparing for college. He had attended various schools in England and Scotland, and then had spent two years in the fashionable Richmond school of Joseph H. Clarke, of Trinity College, Dublin, where he demonstrated considerable facility in Latin, Greek, and declamation. In 1823 he was entered in the well-known school of William Burke, and again was an exceptional student.

Thomas Ellis wrote vividly from his recollection of Poe at this period:

"No boy ever had greater influence over me than he had. He was, indeed, a leader among boys; but my admiration for him scarcely knew bounds; the consequence was, he led me to do many a forbidden thing, for which I was punished. The only whipping I ever knew Mr. Allan to give him was for carrying me out into the fields and woods beyond Belvidere one Saturday, and keeping me there all day until after dark, without anybody at home knowing where we were, and for shooting a lot of domestic fowls, belonging to the proprietor of Belvidere. . . . He taught me to shoot, to swim, and to skate, to play bandy, etc.; and I ought to mention that he once saved me from drowning—for having thrown me into the falls headlong, that I might strike out for myself, he presently found it necessary to come to my help, or it would have been too late."

Poe was fond of sports. One friend of his youth said he was "a swift runner, a wonderful leaper," and "a boxer with slight training." Certainly he was an excellent swimmer; his six-mile swim in the James from Richmond to Warwick, against a strong tide, attests this fact. Robert G. Cabell and Robert Stanard, two of his boyhood chums, accompanied him in a boat or along the bank; Robert Mayo tried to swim the distance with him but gave up at Tree Hill, about halfway. The day was extremely hot, and teen-aged Edgar Poe emerged from the water with blistered face, neck, and back. In later years he wrote concerning this exploit when someone referred to it in the press:

"The writer seems to compare my swim with that of Lord Byron [across the Hellespont], whereas there can be no comparison between them. Any swimmer 'in the falls' in my days would have swum the Hellespont and thought nothing of the matter. I swam from Ludlow's Wharf to Warwick (six miles), in a hot June sun, against one of the strongest tides ever known in the river. It would have been a feat comparatively easy to swim twenty miles in still water. I would not think much of attempting to swim the British Channel from Dover to Calais."

Allowing for a certain amount of braggadocio in the foregoing, the fact remains that Edgar performed an extraordinary feat.

As the well-knit youth of medium height with unusually broad forehead, white skin, and brilliant eyes of hazel gray grew to manhood, his stormy and tragic career began to unfold. During those years he came under the spell of two Richmond women, Jane Stith

Craig Stanard, the inspiration of his memorable poem "To Helen," and Elmira Royster, who may have been his "Lenore."

Jane Stanard was the mother of Poe's friend "Rob" Stanard. She would die insane at thirty in 1824 and her grave is to be seen today in Shockoe Cemetery. But in earlier years the radiant vision of Jane Stanard by the "brilliant widow-niche" of her house on Ninth Street opposite Capitol Square evoked an image in the mind and heart of Edgar Poe that later was made imperishable in one of the world's great lyric poems. Edgar's adoration of Mrs. Stanard was that of a boy barely in his teens for an older married woman. His feeling for Elmira Royster was altogether different.

Jane Stanard's youth had been spent in the home of her parents, the Adam Craigs, at 1812 East Grace Street, one of the two or three oldest houses standing in Richmond in the late twentieth century, and built in the 1780s. As the birthplace of "Poe's Helen," it has an especial attraction and charm.

Poe paid court to Elmira Royster before going off to the University of Virginia at age seventeen. They were engaged when he left for college, she said many years later. During his ten months there he wrote her many letters, all of which were intercepted by her father "because we were too young," Elmira declared. She was sixteen at the time, and hearing nothing from Edgar married A. Barret Shelton the following year. He was older and a person of means and social standing. Some of Richmond's elite regarded Poe slightly askance because his mother had been an actress.

When Poe returned from the university, in December 1826, he was shocked to find that his letters had never reached his fiancée and that their romance was over. Worse still was the growing breach with his foster father, made almost inevitable by the latter's refusal to provide him with the absolute minimum in funds to cover essential expenses at Charlottesville. Allan had been generous in paying for his earlier education in England and Richmond and had often expressed affection for the boy, but he suddenly became parsimonious in the extreme when Edgar entered college. This despite the fact that Allan was then wealthy, whereas he had been badly pressed for money during the depression which struck in 1819.

Allan had no reason to complain of Edgar's scholastic record at the university, for it was excellent. His courses were exclusively in ancient and modern languages. And while there was a great deal of riotous conduct at the institution during that session, and some fifty students sought by the sheriff "traveled off into the woods and mountains, taking their beds and provisions with them"—as Poe put it in a letter to Allan—he himself was not among them. Nor do faculty records indicate that he was guilty of any misconduct at all.

What he did do, as he admitted, was to gamble, in the hope of taking care of his essential university bills, as well as some rather extravagant purchases of clothes. He lost heavily, and some have placed his total indebtedness to students and others at $2,500, but this is probably too high. He also drank at times, and being unusually susceptible to alcohol's effects, he was often thought to have consumed more than was actually the case.

Why Allan became so bitterly hostile to his ward is rather difficult to understand. Poe said his foster father wrote him early in the university session "in terms of the utmost abuse . . . because I could not contrive to pay $150 [in university fees] with $110"— which was all that Allan provided him with when he entered the institution. Granted that Edgar was not without faults, and that he may have done something of which we are not aware, Allan's attitude is a mystery. A possible explanation is that Edgar, who loved Mrs. Allan dearly, found out that Allan was a philanderer. If so, this could have caused his foster father's antagonism. "Jock" Allan sired several illegitimate children by a Mrs. Wills. He provided for them in his will, while leaving Edgar nothing.

Mrs. Allan, the former Frances Keeling Valentine, was a pretty woman of good family, and extremely fond of Edgar. She was understanding and helpful through his many trials. But she was in frail health much of the time and of a nervous disposition. Thus she was unable to counteract the hostility of her domineering husband toward the boy, and Edgar was desperately unhappy. In March 1827, a few months following his return from the university, he enlisted in the United States Army under the name of Edgar A. Perry.

After two years in the service, during which he rose to the highest noncommissioned rank, that of sergeant major, and was unreservedly commended by his superiors, he obtained an honorable discharge.

Toward the end of this period, Mrs. Allan died. Allan refused to finance the boy's education further, and Poe decided to apply for entrance to the United States Military Academy. This was far from being an educational institution congenial to his temperament—he had published two small books of poems while in the army and was determined to publish others—but he was trying to make the best of an unsatisfactory situation. Fortunately, his record in the service was such that he was successful in his application to the Academy.

During his stay at West Point (July 1830 to March 1831), he did well in his studies, was already familiar with the drill from his army experience, and was well liked by the cadets. But creative literary work was virtually impossible, and this was his all-consuming passion. Furthermore, his relations with Allan remained bitter, with no financial support from that quarter.

Poe's letters to his foster father were often movingly pathetic, and Allan failed sadly to appreciate his artistic temperament. At the same time, the older man was understandably infuriated when Poe had the bad taste to write a friend that "Mr. Allan is not very often sober." Poe's letter was forwarded to Allan after Poe reached West Point, and its effect on their already strained relations can be imagined. By this time it was clear that the two men could never be congenial, and while Allan is rightly subject to severe criticism, Poe was by no means blameless.

The youth decided that he must leave West Point, so he got himself dismissed by deliberately disobeying the rules. He went to live in Baltimore with his aunt, Mrs. Maria Poe Clemm, and published a third volume of poems. He also began writing prose tales. But once again he was in tragic circumstances. John Pendleton Kennedy, the Baltimore novelist, came to his aide. "I found him in a state of starvation," Kennedy wrote in his journal after

Poe's death. "I gave him clothing, free access to my table and the use of a horse for exercise." Kennedy was instrumental in obtaining publication of several stories by Poe in the *Southern Literary Messenger* at Richmond. Despite his admiration for Poe, he wrote that the latter was "irregular, eccentric and querulous."

The *Messenger* had been established in 1834 by Thomas W. White, a Richmond printer, for the laudable purpose of raising the level of Southern letters. He himself was without literary ability, but he secured as editorial consultant James E. Heath, a Richmond novelist who later wrote an excellent play. Heath, often called the magazine's "first editor," although he apparently did not actually have the title, served without pay until the following year.

Poe by that time was in correspondence with White concerning work on the magazine. He expressed himself as anxious to return to Richmond, and said he would accept congenial duties on the *Messenger* if the salary were "the merest trifle." John Allan died in 1834, which may have increased Poe's desire to return to the city where he had spent so much of his youth.

The twenty-six-year-old Poe came to Richmond at White's invitation and plunged into his work on the magazine. The *Messenger*'s offices were on the second floor of a building at the southeast corner of Fifteenth and Main. Poe lived in a cheap boardinghouse and was far from happy. He was desperately in love with his thirteen-year-old cousin, Virginia Clemm, and agonizingly fearful that he would lose her. His letter to his Aunt Maria, Virginia's mother, is one of the most moving outpourings that can be imagined. Too long to be reproduced here, it begins, "I am blinded with tears while writing this letter—I have no wish to live another hour. . . . Oh God have mercy on me!" There is much more in this vein. Poe then goes on to say:

"I had procured a sweet little house in a retired section of Church Hill—newly done up with a large garden and every convenience—at only $5 per month. I have been dreaming every day & night since of the rapture I should feel in seeing my only friends—all I love on earth with me there; the pride I would take in making you both comfor[table] & in calling her my wife. But the dream is over. . . . What have I *to live for*? Among strangers with *not one soul to love me*."

At another point Poe says that "every one here receives me with open arms," which hardly comports with his description of himself as "among strangers." However, he was obviously greatly overwrought and apparently on the verge of suicide. Yet the letter does not read as if written by a man under the influence of alcohol, although Poe certainly went on sprees from time to time. There is no reason to believe that he was ever addicted to drugs.

His aunt's reply to his impassioned communication is not of record, but evidently the situation was by no means as hopeless as he feared. For less than a month later he was in Baltimore, at which time a marriage license was taken out for himself and Virginia. The ceremony was not performed until subsequently in Richmond, when another license was issued, but Poe's apprehensions as to Virginia's attitude toward him are seen to have been groundless.

Yet much of the time he was in a state of profound depression, even when he was about to marry Virginia and his fortunes were otherwise greatly improved. "I am wretched and know not why," he wrote his friend John P. Kennedy. "Convince me that it is . . . at all necessary to live."

The fact seems to be, as Poe's finest biographer, Arthur Hobson Quinn, declares, that he was "fighting the most desperate conflict that any man can face, the struggle for sanity." There was mental instability in his family, and he appears to have been aghast at the thought that he might be adjudged insane. It was in an era when "lunatics" were locked up in asylums and forgotten.

Poe was able to persuade his Aunt Maria and Virginia to join him in Richmond, and they were all installed in Mrs. James Yarrington's boardinghouse at Twelfth and Bank Streets, fronting Capitol Square. Board for the three was $9 a week.

Poe's morale was improved by the presence of the ladies, but he was still subject to fits of profound melancholy. He was also being warned by White of the *Messenger* against further drinking. Yet his bouts with the bottle were not as frequent as many suppose. James

Southall Wilson, one of the leading authorities on all aspects of Poe's career, says that "from the summer of 1835 to January, 1837 at most three and possibly only two irregularities from intoxication on Poe's part came to the attention of Thomas W. White." It must be borne in mind, however, that when Poe "fell from the water wagon," he fell with a dull thud. "He was an ill man for days and even weeks," says Wilson.

White warned Poe sternly in September 1835 that should he "again sip the juice," he would be fired. It is difficult to believe that alcohol interfered tremendously with Poe's performance on the magazine, for he was writing all the critical and literary notices, and doing them extremely well. In December White announced that he, White, was being assisted by "a gentleman of distinguished literary talents," and that "journals on every side . . . have rung the praises of his uniquely original vein of imagination, and of humorous, delicate satire."

Poe was, in fact, attracting national attention already with his slashing book reviews and critical articles, as well as with his highly original short stories. In January 1836 he wrote his friend Kennedy in Baltimore, "I am in every respect comfortable and happy." While this euphoria was not to endure, since Poe, like most geniuses, had a mercurial temperament, he was viewing the world through rose-tinted glasses at that particular moment. He mentioned that his annual income from the *Messenger* was $800 and that he had been promised an increase to $1,000.

Poe was married to Virginia in May at Mrs. Yarrington's boardinghouse, and this also helped his morale, at least temporarily. The bride was not quite fourteen, but Thomas W. Cleland, a friend, swore, when a license was obtained, that she was twenty-one. Virginia, though beautiful, was necessarily immature, and she has always remained a somewhat shadowy personality. But Poe loved her devotedly until her death. She was equally steadfast in her love for him.

On their return from from a brief honeymoon in Petersburg, Poe was again absorbed in the *Messenger*. He continued to write criticism, stories, and poems that showed great originality. The magazine's circulation zoomed to about thirty-five hundred, as contrasted with five hundred when he joined the staff. Yet White refused to give him complete control of policy, with the result that Poe was acutely dissatisfied. White reproved him again for drinking. All this combined to cause his resignation in January 1837.

He had been at the helm of the magazine for about eighteen months, and had raised it from a publication of limited reputation to recognition as one of the foremost journals in the land. Poe had written 112 book reviews for the *Messenger*, contributed 8 hitherto unpublished stories, and 7 unpublished poems, while reprinting others. In addition, he handled a considerable correspondence, supervised the make-up of the publication, read proof, and addressed the monthly issues.

As editor of the magazine he did not hesitate to discuss controversial topics of the day. For example, he defended slavery. He also advocated free public education for the state of Virginia, saying that, in view of the absence of public schools, the commonwealth's "once great name is becoming, in the North, a bye-word for imbecility."

Generally speaking, however, Poe's writings, both then and later, were far removed from the contemporary scene. His stories and poems were often concerned with eerie and blood-chilling themes—with, in the words of Van Wyck Brooks, "gloom, despair, sepulchral thoughts, grim fantasies and the fear of impending mental decay." Poe's world was "overhung with the sable wings of lunacy, perversity, hysteria, of sickness, hypochondria, ruin, dissolution and death." He was pathetically neurotic and on the verge of madness at times, especially in his last years. These somber traits may have been, in some degree, inherited, but they certainly stemmed, in part, from the frustrations and torments that beset him during most of his adult life. The normality of his early behavior and his ability to become a sergeant major in the army are in vivid contrast to his later eccentricities and his literary preoccupation with horror, terror, and the grave.

When Poe resigned from the *Messenger* in January 1837, he returned to New York, taking his wife and aunt with him. Mrs. Clemm opened a boardinghouse, and William Gowans, a Scot who spent eight months there, wrote later in praise of Poe's sobriety, hard work, and gentlemanly demeanor during that time. He also described Virginia as "of matchless beauty and loveliness" whose "eye could match that of any houri, and her face deny the genius of any Canova to imitate." Captain Mayne Reed, the novelist, a constant visitor to Poe's home in 1843, described Virginia as "angelically beautiful in person and not less beautiful in spirit. . . . We, the friends of the poet, used to talk of her high qualities." She was then about twenty-one years of age.

The country was in the grip of a depression when Poe went to New York in 1837, and he was unable to obtain steady employment. He accordingly took his family to Philadelphia, in the hope of finding an outlet for his talents. A position on the staff of the *Gentleman's Magazine* became available, and Poe worked there as co-editor for about a year. But he quarreled violently with William E. Burton, the proprietor, and resigned in 1840. Poe had an unfortunate way of making enemies of the very persons who could help him the most. His needlessly sarcastic and biting critiques of books by certain prominent authors are important examples of this.

After leaving the *Gentleman's Magazine*, Poe obtained an editorial position on *Graham's Magazine*, also in Philadelphia. He remained there for slightly more than a year.

During this latter period, in January 1842, his beloved Virginia ruptured a blood vessel while singing at the piano. She lingered for five years, and her life was despaired of on several occasions. The emotional strain on the highly sensitive Poe can be imagined. According to one friend of the family, he contracted "brain fever brought on by extreme suffering of mind and body—actual want and hunger and cold having been borne by this heroic husband in order to supply food, medicine and comforts to his dying wife."

Poe, Virginia, and Mrs. Clemm returned to New York in 1843, with hardly enough money to pay the railroad fare. Virginia finally died in January 1847, in their cottage at Fordham. Poe's drinking seems to have been understandably greater during this period.

He visited Richmond briefly in 1848, for the first time in more than a decade. Hardly anything is known of his movements. A near-duel with John M. Daniel, the fiery editor of the Richmond *Examiner*, was a highlight of his stay, but the circumstances of this encounter are vague.

Poe came back to Richmond the following summer for the final visit of his life and lodged at the Swan Tavern. Whereas he was said by John R. Thompson, editor of the *Southern Literary Messenger*, to have gone on a prolonged drinking bout during his sojourn the year before, this time he joined the Sons of Temperance and, except for two reported lapses, apparently remained sober.

The now famous poet was received with marked enthusiasm and generous hospitality. Robert Stanard, Robert Cabell, and Robert Sully, his boyhood friends, greeted him warmly. Susan Archer Talley, later Mrs. Louis Weiss, saw him on several occasions at Talavera, her parents' farmhouse which many years later became 2315 West Grace Street—still standing in 1976. Talavera, in 1849, was in the suburbs, as was nearby Duncan Lodge, the home of the Mackenzies. Mrs. Weiss wrote long afterward that Poe "spent his mornings in town, but in the evenings would generally drive out to Duncan Lodge [which stood on West Broad Street between today's Lodge and Mackenzie streets]. He liked the half-country neighborhood, and would sometimes join us on our sunset rambles in the romantic old Hermitage grounds." Mrs. Weiss described in detail a visit by Poe to Talavera in 1849, on a "pleasant though slightly drizzly morning in the latter part of September." They discussed "The Raven" and both agreed that it had imperfections. Susan was emphatic in her criticism of certain phrases.

Poverty still dogged Poe's footsteps, despite his rising fame. He wrote Mrs. Clemm, "I have been invited out a great deal—but could seldom go, on account of not having a dress coat."

A "large and enthusiastic" audience greeted him at the Exchange Hotel on August 17, when he lectured on "The Poetic Principle" and read "The Raven." Admission was only twenty-five cents, so that the receipts cannot have added up to much. However, Poe was so strapped for funds that any small sum was welcomed. "I *never* was received with so much enthusiasm," he wrote Mrs. Clemm. "The papers have done nothing but praise me before the lectures and since." He delivered the lecture in Norfolk, to applause, and then returned to Richmond and repeated it. There was general agreement that Poe's voice as a lecturer was exceptionally melodious and had an indefinable quality that gave it a special charm.

During his last visit to Richmond he renewed his courtship of Elmira Royster Shelton, then a widow. The forty-year-old Poe, whose letters to Elmira from the University of Virginia nearly a quarter of a century before had been intercepted, pressed his suit with renewed ardor. The widow Shelton lived at 2407 East Grace Street, a house standing in 1976. During the early part of his visit to Richmond, Poe was often seen mounting the steps to Elmira's front door. Then for several weeks the visits ceased mysteriously, only to be resumed in September. He spent the evening of September 26 at Elmira's, but was not feeling well. She was not engaged to him at the time, she said years afterward, but they had "an understanding." Poe thought they were going to be married.

Despite his malaise, he left for Baltimore by boat the following morning, expecting to return. His subsequent movements are altogether mysterious. He dropped out of sight for six days, and was found semiconscious near a Baltimore polling place where an election was being held. His clothing had been stolen and he was wearing shoddy garments. Poe was taken to a hospital, where he died on October 7. His last words were "God help my poor soul."

Thus ended the star-crossed career of perhaps the most tragic figure in Richmond's history. Born in Boston because his actor-parents happened to be in that city, he called himself "a Virginian" and regarded Richmond as "home." James Southall Wilson said he had "the most brilliant and variously gifted mind that America had yet produced . . . of enormous energy and creative fire." Despite poverty, ill-health, and long-continued emotional strain, he produced in two decades about seventeen volumes. They include some of the loveliest lyric poems and most original short stories in the language, together with a great body of incisive critical writing. Conan Doyle termed him "the inventor of the detective story." Poe's ingenuity and imagination were matched by his exquisite choice of words, words as musical as the notes of a symphony. His prose often gives forth the sounds of poetry, and the names of the characters in his writings have a flowing and rhythmic quality—Ligeia, Israfel, Lenore, Ulalume, and Annabel Lee.

Edgar Allan Poe was at times his own worst enemy, for like many greatly gifted men he was temperamental and unstable. Yet the creative passion within him was never quenched, and he left a literary legacy that will live.

The Decline of Virginia
(1971)

Virginia in the mid-nineteenth century was far less influential in the councils of the South and the nation than it had been a few decades previously. From the predominant place that it had occupied since colonial times, the Old Dominion slipped almost suddenly into a secondary role. What is the explanation?

Several reasons may be advanced. One of them is the drain of thousands of Virginia's ablest and most adventurous sons and daughters, mainly to the less developed regions of the South and West. No fewer than 388,000 former citizens of the commonwealth were living in other states by 1850. Only 949,000 white and free colored people were still in Virginia. Since most of the emigrants left their communities to build new homes under actual or virtual frontier conditions, they tended to be the younger and more vigorous elements.

Among them were many men who later became famous, men whom Virginia could ill afford to lose. Richard Beale Davis has examined this list of expatriates and has come up with the astonishing fact that at least 227 men born in Virginia prior to 1810 served in Congress from other states. There were also such eminent persons as President William Henry Harrison, Stephen F. Austin, founder of Texas, and Sam Houston, its first president; Henry Clay, leader in Congress for decades, secretary of state, and candidate for president; William H. Crawford, senator, cabinet member, and presidential candidate; John Penn and George Walton, signers of the Declaration of Independence from North Carolina

From *Virginia: The New Dominion* (Garden City, N.Y.: Doubleday and Co., 1971).

and Georgia respectively; Ephraim McDowell, pioneer in abdominal surgery; Cyrus McCormick, inventor of the mechanical reaper; nine governors of states and twelve governors of territories, to give only a partial list.

Virginia was not only losing large numbers of valuable citizens, but the state's rank in population was declining steadily. Until 1820, Virginia had the largest population in the Union, but in that year it fell to second place, and by 1860 had skidded to fifth. There were twenty-three members of Virginia's congressional delegation in 1810, but only eleven in 1860.

Why were Virginians leaving in such large numbers, while hardly anybody was moving into the state? One reason was that ours was a young and fast-growing country, and the future in the newly discovered regions of the South and West, with their virgin lands, seemed well-nigh limitless. By contrast, the lands in the older sections of Virginia were becoming, or had become, exhausted.

They were exhausted largely because of the concentration on tobacco as the principal crop. It was a crop which depleted the soil rapidly, and since few people in that era had the least inkling of scientific farming methods, the results were catastrophic. Traveler after traveler in the Tidewater and Piedmont areas in the early years of the nineteenth century reported depressing scenes. The observations of Stephen Ravenel of South Carolina were typical. He was shocked to see "the slovenly farming, the unpainted houses and the ignorance of the lower classes." He added that the latter "are brutish in their manners and exceedingly vulgar . . . and in many instances can neither read nor write."

The general economic downtrend in Virginia was reflected in the sad decline of the College of William and Mary, which had experienced a drastic drop in enrollment, its buildings in a serious state of disrepair. South Carolina, on the other hand, was enjoying exceptional prosperity, owing to the boom in cotton, and this was to continue until the panic of 1819, which hit both South Carolina and Virginia. However, the Carolina planters managed to achieve a higher level of prosperity than those in Virginia until the Civil War.

The economic decline of Virginia was in some degree attributable to the aftermath of the Revolution. Many of the principal planters had been ruined by the war, and there had been considerable devastation in certain areas. Abolition of entails and primogeniture and disestablishment of the Anglican Church added to the general disorganization. Jefferson, Madison, and Monroe were all in straitened circumstances in the first quarter of the nineteenth century. Some of this may well have been due to their rather extravagant and wasteful mode of living, but the economic climate played a part.

In the North there was much greater prosperity and a better living standard throughout the population. Lucian Minor of the William and Mary faculty took a trip to southern New England in the 1830s and contributed a series of articles to the *Southern Literary Messenger*. He wrote from Northampton, Massachusetts: "Here is not a hundredth part of the abject, squalid poverty that our state presents. I have not seen a log house in New England; nor a dwelling house without one or more glass windows. And nine-tenths of the common farm houses are painted." At the end of his journey Minor declared: "No other six weeks of my life have compressed into them half so much excitement, or half as much interest. Those Northern states have very much the start of us Virginians in almost all the constituents of civilization. . . . They . . . possess better organized social and civil institutions. Their usages are more favorable to health, to virtue, to intelligence—and in their thorough, practical understanding of the word COMFORT . . . they are as far before us as we are before the Hottentots or Esquimaux."

Henry Ruffner, president of Washington College, expressed similar sentiments in 1847, when he said in an address, later published as the famous "Ruffner Pamphlet":

"In the free states are seen all the tokens of prosperity. . . . In the older parts of the slave states are seen, on the contrary, too evident signs of stagnation or of positive decay—a sparse population—a slovenly cultivation spread out over vast fields that are wearing out, among others already worn out and desolate; villages and towns 'few and far between,' rarely growing, often decaying, sometimes mere remnants of what they were . . . ; generally no manufactures, not even trades, except the indispensable few—commerce and navigation abandoned, as far as possible, to the people of the free states; and generally, instead of the stir and bustle of industry, a dull and dreamy stillness, broken, if broken at all, by the wordy brawl of politics."

The slave system was responsible for much of this backwardness. Slave labor was much less efficient than free labor. This was due, in part, to the fact that the slave usually had no incentive to work hard. On a few plantations there were rewards for slaves who performed well, but the average chattel was inclined to work as little as possible. He knew that he was a slave for life, anyway. So long as he could escape punishment for failure to perform his task, he saw no advantage in excessive effort.

Virginians were not only moving out of the state; they were also moving across the mountains into the western regions of the Old Dominion, where slaves were comparatively few. The census of 1850 showed that the white population west of the Blue Ridge was 90,000 greater than east of the range. And the people of southwest and northwest Virginia—now West Virginia—were often of fine Anglo-Saxon stock, proud and self-reliant and superior to the brutish type of eastern "poor white" described by Stephen Ravenel. There were "poor whites" in the mountains and valleys of the west, squatting on land they did not own, but the percentage was relatively small. The western Virginians were often self-respecting homeowners, living in their cabins or on their small farms, and asking no help from anyone.

Not only did slavery provide an inefficient system of labor, but the attacks on it from the North seemed to force Virginia and the rest of the South into a perennial posture of defense. In a period when New England was being swept by new ideologies and much of Europe was challenged by philosophical idealism, Virginia's thinking was largely static. Defense of the *status quo* against outsiders became the chief concern of nearly all the leaders.

Youthful Jesse Burton Harrison, just back from Germany in the early 1830s, saw that Virginia needed to stop defending slavery and to get on with a plan for abolishing it. He published a reply in

1832 to Thomas R. Dew's defense of the institution. Harrison advocated a more forward-looking attitude on the part of Virginians who, he said, were too much inclined to bask in the glories of their forebears, instead of carrying the Old Dominion onward to new greatness. He also deplored what he felt to be the excessive desire of young Virginians to rush into politics. Harrison called, furthermore, for reform of the state's archaic system of education.

Backwardness in primary and secondary education—although not at the college level—accounted for much of Virginia's lack of advancement. In the words of the French historian and geographer, Jean Gottmann, the failure of Virginians "to maintain their eighteenth-century leadership in the nation was to a large extent due to the feeble numbers of their educated elite." The percentage of illiteracy among whites in 1850 was 8.6, and only five of the thirty-one states had worse ratings. In 1845, Governor James McDowell, one of the most earnest advocates of better schools, called the situation "absolutely appalling." He referred to "the ruinous process of depopulation and impoverishment now at work," and said it would continue unless the legislature revised, amended, and enlarged the state's "system of education and internal improvement." His plea was largely in vain.

Had it not been for certain spectacular advances in agriculture, Virginia's overall retrogression would have been worse. Thanks to the ingenuity and leadership shown by several individuals, exhaustion and erosion of the soil were checked, and by 1850 there was a distinct upturn in the general level of farming.

Fielding Lewis, who married George Washington's sister, had been an early pioneer in the application of lime to Virginia's soil. John Alexander Binns of Loudoun County had used deep plowing, combined with the application of gypsum to the soil, to restore Loudoun's depleted lands, and had made the county the most productive in the state. The use of gypsum spread rapidly, and Avery O. Craven says in his trail-blazing work, *Soil Exhaustion as a Factor in the Agricultural History of Virginia and Maryland, 1606–1860*, that from 1800 to 1820 "no other single factor made such great changes for the better in the agricultural life of the two states."

Confederate trench, near Richmond

Robert E. Lee Statue, Monument Avenue, Richmond

View from Main Street, Richmond

Ruins of Tredegar Iron Works, Richmond

John Marshall House, Richmond

St. John's Church, Richmond

Virginia State Capitol, Richmond

Shenandoah Valley, from Swift Run Gap

Then came the researches and writings of John Taylor of Caroline, "the philosopher of political agrarianism." His contribution to better farming in the state was deemed the most important made by any individual up to that time. Taylor stressed the principle that "fertility of soil alone can give success." This could be achieved, he said, by "the return of manures of all kinds, animal and vegetable." In his influential book, *Arator* (1813), he advocated deep plowing and crop rotation.

Edmund Ruffin was Virginia's next agricultural pioneer, and his was the most far-reaching contribution of all. His *Essay on Calcareous Manures* (1832) caused a virtual revolution in farming practices in Virginia. In it he emphasized the significance of marl in the restoration of worn-out lands. John Rolfe had drawn attention to the properties of marl more than two centuries before, but Ruffin roused Virginians to a realization of its valuable qualities. His *Essay* ran through five editions, and the Year Book of the U.S. Department of Agriculture for 1895 called it "the most thorough piece of work on a special agricultural subject ever published in the English language." In 1833, Ruffin founded the *Farmer's Register*, a monthly journal designed to disseminate his ideas. It was termed by John Skinner, first editor of the *American Farmer*, "the best publication on agriculture which this country or Europe has ever produced." Ruffin is also authoritatively declared to have "a good claim to being called the father of soil chemistry in America." Ruffin, unfortunately, became involved in a bitter controversy with the bankers of the state after he had suffered financial losses in the panic of 1837. A man of strong, even violent, views on some subjects, he accused the bankers of "the tyranny of avarice, moral fraud and legalized swindling." This stirred up such a storm and caused so many cancellations of subscriptions to the *Farmer's Register* that he decided to stop publishing it in 1842. That, incidentally, was the year after the *Southern Planter* made its initial appearance, to continue in operation for more than a century and a quarter.

Ruffin contended in 1853 that properly marled land in Virginia had increased in value 200 percent. While marl was undoubtedly due a large share of the credit for the great improvement noted in Virginia farming during the 1850s, the at least equally significant role of Peruvian guano should by no means be overlooked. Willoughby Newton, a leading citizen of Westmoreland County, pioneered in introducing this fertilizer to Virginia, and the results were sensational. Newton stated that the introduction of guano "was an interposition of Providence to save the country from total ruin." Guano was relatively expensive, whereas marl was ready to hand and cheap, but those who could afford the Peruvian fertilizer profited greatly from its application to exhausted lands. The farmers of Northern Neck, fellow citizens of Willoughby Newton, were said to have become the richest agricultural population in America.

Thanks to the various innovations, such as the introduction of gypsum, marl, and guano and the organization of agricultural societies to promote their use, soil exhaustion ceased to be a major problem in Virginia in the years immediately preceding the Civil War.

Diversification of crops and the raising of livestock for sale also were important factors in the rise of Virginia farming. Truck crops were grown in lower Tidewater, especially for export to the North. The growing of grain reached such proportions that, except for tobacco, it became Virginia's chief source of farm income. Orchards were planted in the Shenandoah Valley and the Piedmont.

Colonies of farmers came down from the North in the 1840s and 1850s and settled in a number of counties, ranging from Fairfax on the Potomac to the Tidewater counties of the southeast. The Fairfax colony received special attention and was the subject of a series of laudatory articles in the Richmond *Whig* and other papers in 1845. The series was by Samuel Janney of Loudoun, a Quaker who had long agitated against slavery. He pointed to the greatly superior farming methods of the "Yankees," who relied on scientific techniques, crop rotation, and—last, but not least—free labor. The abandoned farms of Fairfax were soon producing in great variety and abundance, and land values skyrocketed.

Janney drew the probably sound conclusion that free labor was largely responsible, and he added that slavery ought to be abolished, so that the "retrograde movement which has so long been going on in the Eastern part of the state" might be arrested. Such a conclusion, in the climate of opinion then existing, was received with a decided lack of enthusiasm, to put it mildly. The Richmond *Examiner*, which had joyfully hailed the coming of the Northerners some years before, now sang a quite different tune. The editor was opposed to this "Vandal invasion of Virginia" with its "fragrant hordes of adventurers fresh from the . . . codfisheries of the Bay State" who would convert areas of the commonwealth into "a paradise of onions, squashes, string beans and 'liberty.'"

Manufacturing, like farming, experienced a decided upturn in Virginia in the 1850s. The Old Dominion had 4,841 manufacturing establishments in the final years of the decade—fifth among all the states and first in the South. New York, Pennsylvania, Ohio, and Massachusetts were still far ahead, but Virginia was making a definitely better showing. In the South, the state ranked number one in several categories, and it led the nation in tobacco manufacture. Richmond led the cities of the world in flour milling. The Tredegar Iron Works at Richmond was the foremost southern industrial establishment in the field. Norfolk, Petersburg, Lynchburg, and other centers of population experienced a factory boom. The hiring of slaves by these factories increased, and this served as an outlet for the state's slave surplus. A greater outlet was in sales of slaves to the Deep South, where the demand remained high.

But despite the manufacturing and farming upturn of the eighteen-fifties, Virginia remained far behind states which, in earlier days, had been far behind Virginia. Examples were given by Governor Joseph Johnson in his message to the General Assembly in 1855:

"At the period of the War of Independence, the commerce of Virginia was four times larger than that of New York. In 1853, the import of the latter amounted to the enormous sum of one hundred and eighty millions yearly, while those of Virginia were not quite $400,000. And during that year, there were cleared from her [New York's] ports 9950 vessels to foreign ports, while from Virginia during the same period 292, and the amount of goods imported was less than four million dollars."

Governor Johnson went on to declare that Virginia's grievous decline could not be ascribed to superior natural advantages elsewhere, since "Virginia has greatly the advantage over any portion of the North in all the elements requisite to constitute a commercial and prosperous community." He added sadly that "like the unfaithful servant, she has failed to improve the talent entrusted to her care."

The inability of leading Virginians, especially those in Richmond, Petersburg, Fredericksburg, and Alexandria, the "river towns," to grasp the vital necessity for developing railroads, is offered by some as an explanation for the failure of Norfolk to realize its potential as a great port. As Thomas J. Wertenbaker puts it in his history of Norfolk:

"Had Virginia . . . placed her dependence upon railways and laid out a wise and comprehensive scheme of construction, how different would have been her history! Instead of squandering millions on unwise projects her outlay would have been returned many times over in increased commerce and manufactures; instead of rushing to disunion, she would have bound her western counties with bands of economic interest. . . . Starting with Norfolk, the state's only great ocean port, a railway should have been built west to Petersburg, Richmond, Charlottesville, Staunton, Charleston and the Ohio River. . . . Then the north and south lines could have been added. . . . Had this been done the products of all Virginia . . . would have poured through this system down to Norfolk. . . . But this was not to be. The fall line towns would not consent to connecting Norfolk with the back country. Having developed under the old system of river navigation, they were determined to maintain their ascendancy by legislative action."

Wertenbaker concedes, however, that the great success of the Erie Canal in New York could well have brought to the "river towns" the sincere conviction that equal success might be obtained in Virginia by developing the James River and the Kanawha Canal, rather than the railroads. The fact remains that Virginia failed to advance commercially and industrially with anything like the speed that might reasonably have been expected. The same is true of the port of Norfolk, which never came close to realizing its potential in the antebellum years.

Virginia not only remained far behind the northern states in the various categories of material and cultural advancement; it also lost the leadership of its own region to South Carolina. From the mid-1830s onward, Charleston rather than Richmond became the center from which emanated the prevailing views of Southerners on most issues of the day. Pre-eminent among those issues was slavery, and John C. Calhoun, with his aggressive championship of the "positive good" thesis, was the man to whom the South looked for guidance. There was no one in Virginia who exercised more than a fraction of his influence, and after his death in 1850 his soul went marching on.

South Carolina and Calhoun had set the tone in 1832 with the Ordinance of Nullification, and they soon came to dominate the thinking of the South. The lovely little town of Charleston, dreaming amid its live oaks and magnolias, never had more than 43,000 inhabitants, less than half of whom were white, but it was the powerful citadel of the fiery secessionists. Seldom in history has any small city exercised such influence over the ideas and attitudes of a vast region. The whole state of Virginia could not match it, and the secessionist views of the Carolinians were to prevail, as Virginia's relatively ineffective leaders sought vainly to avoid the holocaust which loomed ahead.

If the Old Dominion had not sustained so tragic a loss of prestige, its more conservative viewpoint might conceivably have prevailed. Peace rather than war might have been the final arbitrament, as intersectional tensions grew ever more ominous, and the sixties neared.

General Lee Takes Command
(1971)

[By the spring of 1862] Manassas was fading into the past and Confederate arms were sustaining a succession of defeats. The one-year enlistments were expiring, and General George McClellan's invasion of Virginia via the Peninsula would soon begin. Lee was the chief mover, in this critical situation, for the enactment of conscription by the Confederate Congress. The provisions of the Conscription Act, when passed, were not as strong as Lee wanted. The upper and lower age limits were eighteen and thirty-five, whereas he preferred forty-five. Owners of twenty or more slaves were exempt, a provision which did nothing to raise the morale of those who owned just a few slaves or none at all, but in fairness it should be said that many large slaveowners enlisted voluntarily and fought well. The law also permitted the hiring of "substitutes," thus making it possible for reluctant warriors to pay somebody else to do their fighting—another highly dubious provision. But with enlistments expiring in a hundred Confederate regiments, the new legislation came just in time to prevent catastrophe, for McClellan was about to march up the Peninsula.

Then, as he was on the point of launching his invasion, a strange Confederate naval vessel, with armorplate made of railroad iron, moved ponderously out of Norfolk toward the Union fleet in Hampton Roads. She was the onetime Federal ship *Merrimack* sunk the year before by the Federals, but now raised by the Confederates, fitted out in this bizarre fashion, and rechristened the *Virginia*. There were several Negro slaves in the crew.

From *Virginia: The New Dominion* (Garden City, N.Y.: Doubleday and Co., 1971).

The massed Union warships, made of wood almost exactly like those that had fought half a century before in the War of 1812, fired broadsides at the intruder, but the cannon shot bounced harmlessly from the *Virginia*'s sloping armorplate. The Confederate ship closed in, rammed and sank the fifty-gun warship *Cumberland*, and then turned and went for the *Congress*. The last-named wooden vessel caught fire from the *Virginia*'s shelling and surrendered. Naval warfare had been revolutionized in a single day, and the navies of the world were suddenly obsolete. There was near panic in the Union Cabinet, and one member predicted that the *Virginia* would be shelling the White House "before we leave this room."

Such mobility on the part of the *Virginia* was impossible, since her slowness of movement was her greatest handicap. Furthermore, her seeming invulnerability was to be countered at once by the timely appearance of another revolutionary vessel, the *Monitor*. This Union ironclad was constructed along different lines. Described as a "cheese box on a raft," the *Monitor* had a revolving turret of iron, and drew only twelve feet of water to twenty-three for the *Virginia*.

When the *Virginia* moved out next morning with a view to wrecking the entire Union fleet, one by one, she found the *Monitor* standing athwart her path. The guns of both ships opened up, but neither was able to damage the other. After two hours of this futile bombardment, the *Virginia* tried unsuccessfully to ram the *Monitor*. Then the Confederate ship sought to move alongside so that her men could board the *Monitor* for hand-to-hand combat. The Federal vessel sheered off and dropped astern. After six hours, during which neither side did any appreciable damage to the other, the *Monitor* moved into water too shallow for the *Virginia* to follow. It was a drawn battle. Yet tactically it was a victory for the Federal ship, since she was still in being, and able to protect the Union fleet from destruction. The *Virginia* still barred McClellan from using the James, but he could proceed with his plans for invasion via the York. Furthermore, the Union blockade, one of the decisive factors in the war, would be drawn ever tighter, strangling the Confederacy by shutting off vital weapons, food, medicines, and other supplies.

As if this wasn't enough bad news, there were the depressing tidings from Shiloh and Island No. 10 in the "West." Then suddenly Confederate hearts were lifted when Longstreet's infantry division and cavalry units under "Jeb" Stuart passed through Richmond en route to join Joseph E. Johnston's defenses on the Peninsula. The bands played "Dixie," and ladies tossed flowers at the mudstained, often shoeless infantrymen. The latter took the daffodils and hyacinths and stuck them in their caps or their rifle barrels, as the crowds thronging the curb cheered, and the men responded with the rebel yell. There was the sound of bugles on the soft spring air as cavalrymen rode down Franklin Street, pretty girls waved handkerchiefs and threw kisses from windows, and the horsemen bowed in graceful acknowledgment. It was April 17, the first anniversary of secession. The enemy soon would be at Richmond's gates and many of the marching, laughing men would die; but violets perfumed the air on that golden morning in 1862, and the city would forget the mud and blood of war in the excitement of the hour.

McClellan was moving slowly toward Richmond, with about 105,000 men. He was informed by intelligence that the Confederates opposing him numbered 200,000, whereas the actual figure was around 85,000. His faulty information was due in large measure to the inept performance of Allan Pinkerton, the famous detective, who was head of the U.S. Secret Service. Thanks partly to this circumstance, the Union commander hesitated to pursue an aggressive plan of attack.

As McClellan neared Richmond, he encountered the always swampy terrain on both sides of the meandering Chickahominy River, and this, added to the almost bottomless mud caused by spring rains on the primitive roads, was a further deterrent. However, Johnston, aware of his own numerical inferiority, retreated before McClellan, until the latter's advance units were within site of Richmond's spires and within the sound of its church bells.

Norfolk, meanwhile, was taken over by the Federals. The virtually surrounded city could not be effectively defended, so it was evacuated. The Navy Yard was burned to prevent its falling into enemy hands, and shipping offshore was also destroyed. The armor-plated *Virginia*, which had made naval history, had to be burned to prevent her capture.

With the loss of this epoch-making vessel, the Confederate Navy was vastly reduced in capability, although Secretary of the Navy Mallory performed prodigies with very little. So did Commander Matthew Fontaine Maury, whose torpedoes were so very effective.

Following loss of the *Virginia*, Confederate fortifications were erected in frantic haste at Drewry's Bluff on the James below Richmond, with a view to preventing a Federal incursion. Federal warships, the formidable *Monitor* among them, steamed up the river on May 15, and opened a bombardment against the unfinished gun emplacements on the heights. The Confederate artillerymen there were devastatingly accurate, and the attackers were driven back downstream.

This gave encouragement to Richmond, as it faced what appeared to be imminent Union assault by land. The Virginia General Assembly voted to put the city to the torch, rather than surrender, and citizens promised to burn their homes. There were plans for firing the Capitol and blowing up the statue of Washington in the square.

Johnston attacked McClellan on May 31. In the ensuing Battle of Seven Pines, Johnston was severely wounded. Jefferson Davis named Robert E. Lee to succeed him in command. It was a turning point in the war, for now the Confederate forces in the Old Dominion would be led by one of history's greatest military geniuses. Lee promptly named the force defending Richmond the "Army of Northern Virginia."

There was no enthusiasm from the Army or the public over the appointment of Lee. He was still under a cloud, as a result of the unfair criticism following his unsuccessful efforts in the western mountains and his unexciting mission to fortify Charleston and Savannah. Not only so, but when he immediately put his soldiers to work building vital fortifications in front of Richmond, he was contemptuously dubbed the "King of Spades." His supposed excess of caution was contrasted with the *élan* and aggressive spirit of "Stonewall" Jackson. Actually, without Lee's masterful overall strategic concepts, Jackson's triumphs in the Valley would have been impossible.

Jackson, at that moment, was leading his troops in one of the most memorable campaigns in the annals of war. In the Shenandoah Valley his half-trained army was outmaneuvering and outfighting much larger Federal forces. Jackson moved with astonishing speed, and always with the element of surprise. In three weeks, from May 19 to June 9, beginning with a force of 6,000 that was never larger than 19,000 he defeated, eluded, or nullified Federal forces totaling 65,000.

Jackson hit Union General N. P. Banks like a thunderbolt at Winchester and drove him all the way across the Potomac, seizing enormous quantities of supplies in the process. This brought such alarm to the United States government that President Lincoln, fearing an attack on Washington, wired McClellan that instructions to McDowell to join him were being countermanded. Those were the reinforcements for which McClellan had long been waiting in front of Richmond, and now they were gone. Jackson had thrown such consternation into the North that Lincoln even withdrew units from McDowell's command near Fredericksburg and sent them chasing the elusive "Stonewall" in the Valley. At the same time, he ordered General J. C. Fremont to assail "Old Jack"—aged thirty-eight—from another direction, while a third Union force was coming at him from still another. Jackson slipped between two of these attacking forces, and on successive days, at Cross Keys and Port Republic, gave each of them a bloody nose.

That ended Federal efforts to trap and smash Jackson in the renowned Valley Campaign—a classic studied in the military academies of the world. "Stonewall's" chief object—to prevent the reinforcement of McClellan by McDowell in front of Richmond—had been accomplished, although he had sustained a great professional and personal loss in the death of General Turner Ashby.

Through it all, the First Brigade was the spearhead of Jackson's lethal thrusts. Called the Stonewall Brigade from the time of its glorious baptism of fire at First Manassas, it was later compared to "the Macedonian Phalanx of Alexander, the Tenth Legion of Caesar, the Paladins of Charlemagne, the Ironsides of Cromwell, and the Old Guard of Napoleon." Its historian, James I. Robertson Jr., terms it with justice "the most renowned [brigade] in Confederate military history." Decimated by casualties during four years of fighting, during which it was usually given the most dangerous and difficult missions, only 210 of its 2,600 original members would stack arms at Appomatox.

Jackson's Valley campaign was barely over when Colonel J. E. B. Stuart electrified the South with one of the most spectacular feats of the war. Lee had instructed him to scout in the rear of the enemy along the Chickahominy. On the morning of June 12, with 1,200 men, including the gigantic Heros von Borcke, the Prussian dragoon who had run the blockade to fight for the Confederacy, Stuart moved. This was no time for flags and bugles, or for the minstrelsy of banjo-thrumming "Joe" Sweeny, who entertained Stuart's men in their lighter moments. Quietly and without fanfare, the horsemen trotted out of Richmond along the Brook Turnpike, and many who saw them guessed that they were heading for the Valley to reinforce Jackson. But they turned eastward beyond Ashland. Occasional enemy pickets were encountered as the scouting force penetrated deep into Union-occupied territory. In Hanover County, Captain William Latané's Essex Light Dragoons collided suddenly with Union calvarymen. There was a sharp fight with sabers and pistols, and Latané was shot dead.

By the time Stuart had reached the vicinity of Old Church, he had gotten the information Lee wanted concerning the Federals. The normal course for Stuart would have been to return to Richmond over the route by which he had come. But the audacious cavalryman decided otherwise. He would ride entirely around McClellan's army and enter Richmond from the east. This he did, past Tunstall, Talleysville, and Charles City Courthouse, across McClellan's lines of communication and through areas where there were scattered units of Union troops and supply depots. He was back in Richmond June 15, bringing 165 prisoners and 260 captured animals—all with the loss of exactly one man, Captain Latané. This amazing feat, combined with the much more far-reaching victories of Jackson in the Valley, brought encouragement to the South at a time when a long series of reverses had greatly damaged Confederate morale.

But Lee, defending Richmond, was facing a force larger than his own—a well-equipped, well-armed, and disciplined host, the most formidable yet put together on American soil. He boldly decided to bring Jackson secretly from the Valley, in an effort to destroy the Union Army. The risks were great, but Lee was never afraid of risks.

Jackson and his assistant adjutant general, Major Robert L. Dabney—an eminent Presbyterian clergyman unaccountably chosen for that post—left for Richmond in a closed railroad car. Getting out at Frederick's Hall they mounted horses after midnight and proceeded to their rendezvous with Lee. Jackson said his men could be in position on McClellan's flank at dawn on June 26, and all plans were made on that assumption. But Jackson and his men failed, for once, to meet a timetable. They were a day late, for reasons not fully explained, and Jackson himself arrived in a state of near-exhaustion from lack of sleep, a situation that would seriously damage his effectiveness throughout the Seven Days' Battles. He actually went to sleep one night at supper with a biscuit in his mouth.

Under these inauspicious circumstances, Lee launched the campaign. It involved battles at Mechanicsville on June 26, Gaines's Mill, June 27, Savage's Station, June 29, Frayser's Farm, June 30, and Malvern Hill, July 1. The muddy terrain along the Chickahominy swamps and in much of the rest of the area was a handicap for both sides, but Lee's maps were inferior to those of the Federals, strange as that must seem. The Federals also had greatly superior artillery and used it more effectively. Lee had to rely heavily on a single factory for his ordnance, the Tredegar Iron Works at Richmond, and such guns as he had were not deployed to the best advantage. Furthermore, Lee lacked an effective general staff.

One result of all this was that in almost every engagement, Lee launched attacks on McClellan at the points and under the circumstances that McClellan preferred. There was the Confederate slaughter when A. P. Hill attacked at Beaver Dam Creek, near

Mechanicsville, on the opening day. There was the even greater slaughter at Malvern Hill on the final day, with similar examples in between.

"Stonewall" Jackson, utterly used up by a series of long, tiring rides to and from the Valley, combined with practically no sleep, was almost wholly ineffective throughout. One result was that Lee's golden opportunity at Frayser's Farm to destroy the Union Army was missed. Jackson, the man whose tremendous drive and dynamism made him a legend on two continents, suddenly seemed almost paralyzed, mentally and physically. He slept under a tree in broad daylight beside White Oak Swamp, instead of rushing to Longstreet's aid. When he woke up, he seemed in a trance, and totally unaware that the last chance to annihilate McClellan was slipping away.

After Malvern Hill—with its dreadful toll of southern youth, who charged fearlessly time and again in the face of massed Federal artillery—the rain came pouring down. Any opportunity that Lee had to pursue the Union Army effectively was made hopeless by the water and mud. McClellan succeeded in getting his battered forces to Harrison's Landing on the James, where, under the protection of Federal gunboats, he could not be reached. The following month, the Union commander abandoned his effort to take Richmond and began moving his troops by water to cantonments near Washington.

Confederate soldiers in bloody bandages had begun pouring into Richmond after the Battle of Seven Pines, and the flow of the wounded and maimed mounted with each engagement. Nearly 16,000 men in Lee's army were wounded during the fighting which began May 31 and ended July 1. By every available means of transport—wagons, ambulances, private carriages, and public hacks—armless men, legless men, men with other dreadful injuries were brought groaning over the rough roads to the huge hospital on Chimborazo Heights, to the great Winder Hospital near the western edge of the city on Cary Street, and to dozens of smaller hospitals. Accommodations were swamped by this deluge of suffering Confederates, and many died for lack of attention. It was nobody's fault. The doctors worked almost around the clock.

The women of Richmond, in particular, were eager to help and zealous in providing all possible comforts, often in their homes. But the need was too great to be met by the available personnel and facilities.

Yet, in the face of many handicaps and obstacles, Richmond had been saved. General Lee was no longer the "King of Spades"; on the contrary he was suddenly the idol of Virginia and the South. Lee's success in driving McClellan from the gates of the Confederate capital combined with Jackson's manhandling of several strong Union forces in the Valley convinced many Virginians that the South could never be defeated.

Charlottesville in the 1910s
(1978)

The inauguration of Woodrow Wilson as president of the United States in 1913 was a major event of my youth. Our troop of Boy Scouts went to Washington "to keep order" along Pennsylvania Avenue, or so it was said. The Reverend Beverley D. Tucker, Jr., rector of St. Paul's Episcopal Church at the university, afterward bishop of Ohio, was our beloved scoutmaster. After we had performed our function, such as it was, in Washington, and the parade and ceremonies had finally ended, we repaired, exhausted, to the Union Station. Our train, like most of the trains, was hours late. So we lay down on the station floor and went to sleep. Suddenly at some time after midnight we were roused and told to board our coach. In a semistupified condition we hurried to the steps leading down to the platform. I was only half awake, and when I reached the top of the stairs I stumbled and fell headlong all the way to the first landing. My fellow Scouts thought I had smashed a few bones, if not my skull, but I seemed in those days to have a genius for falling into ice houses or down flights of steps and emerging unscathed. In this instance, unfortunately, I fell down the wrong steps and had to pick myself up and go back to the right ones. But I arose from my plunge with no breaks or sprains.

However, I must confess that a couple of years before my epoch-making dive in the Washington depot I took another with less satisfactory results. I was galumphing down dusty Rugby Road on Andantino, our somewhat scruffy carriage horse, when

From *Across the Years: Memories of a Virginian* (Garden City, N.Y.: Doubleday and Co., 1978).

he took it into his head to turn abruptly leftward into Gordon Avenue. I was unaware of his intention until it was too late, with the result that I took a header and broke my right arm just above the wrist when I hit the ground. It was soon healed.

I was never a good rider in my youth, and I did no riding at all in later years. My Uncle Staige Saunders, who was a great "kidder," but who knew whereof he spoke in this instance, said my bouncing and jouncing style of riding was such that he could see the Blue Ridge Mountains between me and the horse.

While I am recording my early mishaps of one sort or another, I must mention what happened when I was climbing around on the not quite completed stadium at Lambeth Field. My foot slipped and my mouth came down on the corner of a concrete step. One of my upper front teeth was knocked out, another was cracked, and my lower lip was badly cut. I picked up the tooth from the ground and walked home, bleeding profusely. I must have been a gory sight when I walked into the room where my mother was sitting. She washed the blood from my face, and we drove in the surrey to see Dr. Harry L. Smith, the family dentist. He kept my tooth overnight, and told me to return the next day. At that time he stuck the tooth into my mouth and put a brace on it, in the hope that it would grow back. *Mirabile dictu*, it did, thereby making medical history as of that time. My case was cited for decades in the University of Virginia Medical School. However, I knocked the tooth out several years later playing basketball, so it had to be replaced with an artificial one. The scar where I cut my lip is still there.

My father was wont to remark that he didn't see how boys ever grew to manhood, in view of the manner in which they fell out of trees, off of bicycles or down steps, slashed themselves accidentally with pocket knives, ran around in the cold without proper clothing, experimented with firearms, broke through the ice while skating, and so on.

One perilous pastime of my youth was the shooting off of firecrackers at Christmas and on the Fourth of July. This was legal in those days, and the wonder is that some of us didn't get our hands or fingers blown off. The small firecrackers were not lethally dangerous, but the "cannon crackers" were another story. We would light these and throw them as far as possible before they went off with a reverberating roar. Christmas and the glorious Fourth would not have been half as much fun without them.

I learned to swim at an early age, thanks to my older cousin, Preston Lockwood of St. Louis, who took me to the pool in the basement of the university's Fayerweather Gymnasium for lessons. The pool was dank and dark, and bullfrogs, so the story went, had grown to maturity in its dim recesses. It wasn't long before I was able to paddle around there on my own. When I felt entirely at home in the water, I began going to the old reservoir on the lower reaches of Observatory Mountain near the university. This was the favorite community "swimmin' hole" in summer. It was patronized exclusively by males, including some university students and numerous boys, large and small. It never occurred to us to wear anything while swimming or diving there, despite the fact that the reservoir was only a relatively short distance from the road. It was in the woods, so that the gamboling nudists could not readily by seen. Presumably the ladies of the community who might be taking walks in that area to admire the mountain laurel maintained a discreet distance. They surely must have heard the loud shouting.

A sensation of the year 1910 was Halley's Comet. It completes its circuit every seventy-six years and will be seen again in 1986. This was the comet that flashed alarmingly across the sky late in the year 1606 when the Jamestown settlers were preparing to embark from London to Virginia. Such a portent in that era was supposed to be ominous in the extreme. When Halley's Comet returned in 1910, for its fourth circuit since the 1606 appearance, there was some lurid stuff in the press. Almost anything might happen, it was said, when the earth passed through a million miles of the comet's tail at a speed of 2,500 miles a minute. My parents waked my sister Lucy and me one night and took us out into the yard to view the dazzling celestial phenomenon with its brilliant tail extending across the heavens.

Another excitement was when the circus would come to town. We would go down to Main Street in Charlottesville and wait long hours for the parade to pass. It was always late, but it would finally come into view with its clowns, its beautiful ladies in spangled tights, its ponderous pachyderms, and its fierce animals pacing back and forth in their cages. Always there was one vehicle with its shutters closed to pique the crowd's curiosity. And always, of course, there was the steam calliope bringing up the rear with its shrill tootling.

On a much smaller scale was the divertissement provided when a monkey and organ grinder came occasionally to our neighborhood. This was a rare and unpredictable event, but suddenly in our front yard the organ grinder, usually Italian, would appear with his monkey on a leash. All the kids would rally 'round, and the monkey would gobble a banana or munch an apple, if either was forthcoming, picking fleas from his hide the while. The organ grinder would accept any small coins that were offered and move on down the road.

The newly invented motion pictures were other excitements of the time. A nickel would get you in, if you could dig one up, and another nickel would provide peanuts or candy. A lady played the piano during much of the silent show, but she had to retire periodically to rest. Mary Pickford, Pearl White, House Peters, Charlie Chaplin, Francis X. Bushman, and Theda Bara were among the matinee idols.

The collection of baseball cards (cards that came in packages of certain brands of cigarettes, especially Piedmonts), with pictures of big league baseball players on them, was one of my special interests. I knew the name and batting average of virtually every player in the National and American leagues. Like all such collectors, I sought vainly and constantly for a picture of Honus Wagner, the star shortstop of the Pittsburgh Pirates and the league's leading hitter. We didn't know that Wagner had told the makers of Piedmonts to take him out of their collection since he didn't want to be associated with the sale of cigarettes. A mere handful of the Wagner pictures got into circulation. One of them turned up in 1975, and the finder said he was holding it for $3,000.

Given my interest in the stars of the diamond, it was an annual thrill when the Washington Senators of the American League came to the University of Virginia for early spring training. This lasted only a few years, for the weather there was too uncertain and not warm enough. But I was able to see such immortals as Walter Johnson and Eddy Ainsmith, the famous battery which made baseball history. Ainsmith, a powerful and extremely agile man, caught Johnson for many years. The latter, a tall, broad-shouldered, brawny Kansan with blazing speed, made an amazing record of wins, losses, and strike-outs with the perennially second-division Washington club.

Another early diversion was attendance at the performances of Shakespeare presented by the Ben Greet Players, an English company which provided outdoor plays on college campuses. This was my introduction to Shakespeare on the stage.

Our home, Edgewood, was a hospitable one. My mother, in particular, loved to entertain, and somehow managed to do it constantly, despite our small means. There was almost always a stream of guests, either staying in the house or joining us for meals. Like many Virginia women of her generation, Mother hardly ever entered the kitchen and knew nothing whatever about cooking. She always had a cook to perform that office.

Belles who came to the university dances were frequent guests in our home. Two of the most beauteous and charming were Beatrice ("B") Crawford, later Mrs. Merritt T. Cooke, and Sarah Hamilton, later Mrs. Stephen Booth McKinney. It was nothing to have half a dozen palpitating students in our parlor at one time, sitting figuratively at the feet of one of these beauties. My father used to marvel at the ease with which B Crawford or Sarah Hamilton would make what were called "goo-goo eyes" at each one of the swains in turn, giving each the impression that he was "it," when, as likely as not, none of them was.

There was no such thing in that era as the "going steady" of later years, when a young man and girl would see nobody else for an entire weekend, and also would dance with one another exclusively. By contrast, in the early 1900s there was a constant shifting of dates, and at dances there were cards specifying the youth with whom the girl would start each dance. But then, for the belles a line would form, and there would be a series of "breaks" before the music stopped. In other words, each belle would dance with quite a number of individuals before the next dance on the card came up. Of course there were always a few "sad birds" who got no breaks at all.

A favorite and quite swank method of dating was to hire a horse and buggy from a downtown livery stable. The equipage would be delivered by a young black boy. The lady in the case, perhaps in a "peach basket" hat and wearing a corsage of violets, and her sharply dressed escort, in peg-top trousers and the type of stiff collar later made famous by Herbert Hoover, would climb into the buggy and traverse either the three-mile or the nine-mile circuit—two drives in the vicinity of Charlottesville. Usually the barefoot young black sat on the back of the vehicle throughout the drive, facing the rear with his legs dangling. This last invariably cramped the style of any ambitious suitor.

Ladies were sufficiently daring in about the year 1910 to raise their skirts from the level of the ankle bone to that of the shoe top. Another evidence of advancing civilization was seen when it became possible to use the term "leg" instead of "limb." Then too there was the emergence of the "peek-a-boo waist." It had embroidered perforations which permitted glimpses of female epidermis upon the arms and "as much as two inches below the nape of the neck." Some clergymen were outraged.

Women were not yet smoking in appreciable numbers. In fact, New York City passed a law in 1908 forbidding them to smoke. This caused the *New York Herald* to headline the fact that several women were seen puffing cigarettes in a carriage en route to the opera.

I was not concerned with such matters at that stage of my career, although when I reached my teens I did occasionally puff on corn silk wrapped in a piece of paper—a horrendous smoke which scarified the tongue and couldn't possibly have been anything but an ordeal.

Certain comic strips attracted me, especially one called "Us Boys." Its principal character was Eaglebeak Spruder, a tough guy who wore his cap either backwards or sideways. This seemed to give him a special and indefinable charm.

Scoutmaster Tucker took the university troop on two summer camping trips, lasting about a week, one on the North River near Lexington and the other on the Cowpasture near Millboro Springs. I never got enough to eat on the former trip, and I don't think the others did either. The cuisine was better managed the second time around. A dire calamity on the second trip occurred when Hippo Minor, who in his early years was vastly overweight, got the worst case of poison oak I ever saw. We fished and swam and took hikes both years, and the Cowpasture seemed to me, at age thirteen, to be a powerful and impressive stream. What was my astonishment when I saw it some forty years later, and found it to be hardly more than a good-sized creek.

For ten straight years, from 1907 to 1917, I spent part of each summer at oak-shaded Caryswood, the farm of my great-uncles and -aunts near Evington, Virginia, a small hamlet on the Southern Railway some eighteen miles below Lynchburg. The house was built in the 1850s.

Getting to Evington from Charlottesville was, in itself, an adventure. I always traveled in the reeking, cinder-strewn day coach, and my rations were a couple of hard-boiled eggs, plus maybe a sandwich and a chicken drumstick and gizzard. The highlight of the trip was the tunnel just outside of Lynchburg. I usually choked on the smoke, but there was a thrill in passing through the murky tube.

I was one of four boys, all cousins, who sojourned together at Caryswood, and our simple bucolic amusements and diversions doubtless have little appeal for the younger generation today. We cut "bee trees" to get the honey, gigged frogs, went 'coon hunting—but usually caught only 'possums—made cider, filled mudholes in the country road with rocks, swam "nekkid" in Flat Creek, and played tennis on a "court" which was merely a level place on the front lawn with a net stretched across it. Since there were no backstops, we must have chased those tennis balls thousands of miles.

John Staige Davis, my cousin from the university, and Edward Hickson, a relative from South Carolina, were two of the quartet of boys at Caryswood, and William H. Irvine, later a leading member of the Virginia House of Delegates, was the other. Edward Hickson has practiced medicine for many years at Rustburg, the county seat of Campbell County, in which Caryswood is located.

We boys slept in the two-story "office" in the yard, along with Uncle Staige Saunders, a delightful bachelor who ran the farm. He was on the first floor and we on the second. Our sleeping was done on two hard double beds, with mattresses made of something closely resembling bricks or paving blocks. We scorned the effete facilities of the big house, and used the privy behind the barn. Since there was no tub or shower in the office, our ablutions were performed in one of the various swimming holes, albeit without soap.

Uncle Staige dubbed us boys "professors," and provided each of us with a "chair." I was libelously charged with bathing less often than I should, so I became "Professor of Conservation of Natural Resources."

The professors engaged in activities which might seem to their counterparts today to be worse than useless. For example, we decided that we would walk to Lynchburg, which is twenty miles by road. We didn't intend to do anything spectacular after we got there, but we set forth at dawn. At about midday we arrived, went to two movie shows and caught the train back to Evington.

On another occasion we organized a camping and fishing expedition to Otter River, some six or eight miles distant. Our wagon train was a formidable one, and after hours of arduous travel, we reached a swampy portion of the stream. But before we could hook a single catfish, squadrons of mosquitoes approximately the size of turkey buzzards descended upon us and began operating on the exposed portion of our anatomies. We spent a miserable night, amid the whining of those dive bombers, and returned, scratching violently, to Caryswood.

The hay loft under the roof of the Caryswood barn was among our regular hangouts. John Staige Davis went to sleep there in broad daylight and slid, snoring, down the hay pile and through the outside door of the second floor. He hit the ground with a thud—apparently on his head. We assured him that if he ever committed, say, an ax murder, he could count on us to testify that his brain had been heavily damaged in his youth.

Automobiles were nonexistent in the Caryswood area for the greater part of the decade when I was a sojourner there. We traveled the three miles to Evington on horseback, in a buggy or a wagon, or on our feet, which were always bare until about the year 1913. The trip took most of the morning or afternoon. The rutted country road passed through a number of farms, and several gates had to be opened and shut, lest the bulls wander or the billy goats stray. When we got to Evington we collected the mail and usually dropped in at one of the two small stores for a bottle of pop and to hear the latest gossip. After sixty years I can still smell the pungent odor that permeated those premises, a combination of chewing tobacco, leather, rubber, and cheap candy.

Generally speaking, we boys did not use the "big house," except at meals. These powerful and greatly relished repasts were enlivened by the napkin-ring sharpshooting of Uncle Staige. Everybody had a napkin ring in those days, and while the table was being cleared for dessert, Uncle Staige would collect the rings and begin trying to make one after another jump over the flowers in the center. His technique was to press down on the ring with his forefinger, thus causing it to bound upward. Aunt Mary, at the other end of the table, always shook her head sternly in disapproval but with scant results.

Nobody fires napkin rings across the table at Caryswood anymore, for the old place was sold when the last of the Saunderses died. It looks much as it did half a century ago, although the coming of the motor age has wrought important changes. Whereas in earlier days the dirt road crossed the lower part of the yard, and neighbors or transients would exchange greetings from their surreys, buggies, or wagons, the modern hard-surface highway is farther from the house and out of sight of the front porch.

But while the aforesaid friendly neighborliness is missed, Evington and Caryswood have been brought much closer together, and places that were almost inaccessible are now within easy motoring distance. It is no longer necessary to drive through cow pastures, opening and shutting gates, and the trip from Caryswood to Evington, which took about an hour in earlier times, can now be made in about four minutes. We have here in microcosm the transformation that has taken place throughout most of America.

Yet as I look back across the years, I see four boys—hatless, coatless, and shoeless—strolling down a winding lane, making footprints in the dust.

A Prophet of the New South
(1929)

Along Richmond's Main Street there is the clanging of trolley cars and the honking of trucks and automobiles. Formerly one of the fashionable thoroughfares in the languid old city by the James, it is no longer the habitat of what are sometimes called the First Families of Virginia. Among the great figures of the past whose homes were on Main Street was Edgar Allan Poe, who lived with his foster father, John Allan, at Main and Fifth. That was a century ago, and the house is no longer standing.

However, there still remain on the street a few of the stately mansions of an earlier day. True, most of them are falling into decay, but they stand, nonetheless, as mute witnesses to a vanished past—as relics of an epoch when Patrick Henry hurled defiance in the teeth of George III; when John Marshall was Richmond's First Citizen; or when Robert E. Lee lived on East Franklin Street and the jaunty panache of gallant "Jeb" Stuart caused the hearts of Richmond belles to palpitate beneath their crinolines.

But if this once aristocratic thoroughfare today has been abandoned almost entirely to the uses of commerce and to cheap houses for workingmen, it still prides itself on the possession of one of the most charmingly picturesque of antebellum homes. At the corner of Foushee and Main streets, behind an old iron fence, framed in magnolias and ancient box bushes and almost totally out of keeping with its surroundings, stands a lovely gray-walled building of Georgian design. Here, since girlhood, has lived Ellen Glasgow, one of the two writers of international reputation of whom the former Confederate capital can boast.

From the *New York Herald Tribune*, August 25, 1929.

The shoddiness of the neighborhood contrasts alarmingly with the scrupulous neatness of the shrubs behind the fence and the well-kept appearance of the great house itself, with its shiny brass knocker and doorknob and its trim window boxes. Two doors away is a garage and immediately opposite is a church. It was erected by Episcopalians and was used by them for many years, but the members moved away from that part of the city in such large numbers that the church building was sold not long ago to an obscure evangelical sect.

A facetious policeman recently remarked to Miss Glasgow that her home is situated "near the heart of the bootlegging district." She replied laughingly that she regarded it as something of an admission for an officer of the law to acknowledge that Richmond has a bootlegging district and that, anyway, she is comforted by the reflection that even a bootlegging district has a heart!

Thus, undisturbed by the unprepossessing nature of the neighborhood or by the immediate proximity of bootleggers, the South's most important woman novelist continues to live under her ancestral roof tree. And let it be noted that not until she had lived there for forty-five years and had published fourteen novels, a book of short stories, and a volume of poems did Richmond become fully aware of her presence.

Prior to the appearance of *Barren Ground*, in 1925, Miss Glasgow was accepted by the city more or less as a matter of course. Her books were regarded by the vast majority of Richmonders as quite safe and quite sane, inculcating no dangerous or seditious doctrines and meeting to a satisfactory degree the conservative requirements of the United Daughters of the Confederacy. But with the publication of *Barren Ground* Richmond in particular and the state of Virginia in general began to awaken to the fact that heterodoxy had arisen in their midst.

Here was a lady of impeccable lineage, who had received a proper Christian upbringing in one of the city's most aristocratic homes, but who was manifestly breaking with the Southern literary tradition. Her latest book, they reasoned, was certainly far removed in spirit from the unimpeachable standard set for Southern novelists by Thomas Nelson Page, James Lane Allen, and Francis Hopkinson Smith. Surely there was nothing so unpleasantly realistic in *Marse Chan*, *The Choir Invisible*, or *Colonel Carter of Cartersville*. They shook their heads sadly and wondered what it could mean.

The commotion occasioned by the appearance of *Barren Ground* had scarcely died down when the First Families were rudely jarred again, this time more severely than before. Needless to say, it was *The Romantic Comedians* which caused the second upheaval in the best Richmond circles. Elderly ladies and gentlemen, reared in the great tradition and accustomed to being treated with the respect to which their family trees entitled them, were shocked to find themselves, in the persons of Amanda Lightfoot and Judge Honeywell, irreverently dissected and held up to ridicule before the public gaze.

Not only this, but, incredible as it seemed, Ellen Glasgow was actually seeking to undermine their carefully treasured and long-cherished conviction that the universe should properly revolve about one's ancestors, the traditions and customs of the Old South, and the Episcopal Church. Such audacity really was beyond the pale. The fact that the critics hailed her book as one of the most delicious social satires of the age made Miss Glasgow's sin all the more heinous. She, a member of an old Virginia family, had given the Judas kiss to her own people. They felt that they had been betrayed in the house of their fathers.

But, heavy as was this cross, their troubles were not yet over. Three years passed, and they had recovered moderately well from the disconcerting effects of *The Romantic Comedians* when there burst upon them one day this month another devastating satire, *They Stooped to Folly*. Miss Glasgow had stirred up the animals again. Her latest book was even more merciless than its predecessor in its treatment of once sacred topics. Once more there was indignation on the part of the orthodox.

Thus it should be fairly obvious that Richmond is at last fully aware of Ellen Glasgow. After regarding her for a quarter of a century with almost unruffled complaisance, it now views her with perturbed attention. Having been shocked thrice consecutively in late years, the city has learned to await the appearance of her novels with a certain nervous expectancy. And with good reason. For few indeed there are who can face a barrage of Miss Glasgow's crackling epigrams and mordant wit and come through the bombardment unscathed. No living American writer is more adept at puncturing a hollow pretense with a single neatly turned phrase or more clever at hitting off the foibles of an entire stratum of society in a few words of epigrammatic brilliance.

It is rather amusing, however, that Richmond, and the rest of the United States as well, has been so slow to realize that the author of *The Battleground* and *The Voice of the People* is in revolt against the established order. From the very outset of her literary career she has sought to break with convention, but until 1925 only a small minority inside or outside Virginia was conscious of the fact.

For example, her first published work, a story entitled "A Woman of Tomorrow," which she sold to *Short Stories* for fifteen dollars when she was only fifteen years of age, embodied what was at that time a highly advanced feminist point of view, but apparently nobody knew what she was talking about. The same thing, with incidental variations, has been true of virtually all her books, both prose and poetry. In each of them she has sought to wage war on sentimentality, to shatter the chivalric tradition and to win intellectual emancipation for her sex.

But the fact that her writings represented a protest against what is termed the "nightingale and 'yes massa'" type of fiction was lost on her readers for many years. In her only book of verse, published in 1902, she proclaimed that she had discovered "the freedom of despair," but although this was a doctrine utterly out of keeping with the period, no one appeared to find her statement of it especially subversive. When *Virginia*, which she regards as one of her best novels, made its appearance in 1913, it embodied an ironic picture of man's ideal of woman, according to Victorian standards, but Miss Glasgow declares that at the time nobody had any idea what she was driving at. As stated above, it was not until the publication of *Barren Ground*, which, incidentally, is Miss Glasgow's favorite among all her novels, that the reading public awoke to her real significance.

In view of the foregoing, it is needless to point out that the author of *They Stooped to Folly* and eighteen other books dealing with Southern life is intensely interested in the "New South" in all of its varied manifestations. Indeed, she is one of its major prophets, and it is but natural that she should regard it as superior in some respects to the Old South, although she is fully aware that the South of today is largely lacking in some of the elements which gave the antebellum South its greatest charm.

She declares that she could never have been satisfied to live below the Mason and Dixon line in the palmy days of the great tradition, because of the restrictions with which her sex then was hemmed about. Of course, these restrictions continued until well into the twentieth century, but they have at last been annihilated and woman, North and South, is now completely emancipated. Miss Glasgow feels, too, that the South of today is more vital and alive than ever before. Some years ago she paraphrased Bismarck by declaring that a paramount need of the region below the Potomac was "blood and irony." By this she meant that it should have an infusion of red fighting blood which would reinvigorate the blue and somewhat anaemic liquid which was then coursing through Southern veins, and that at the same time Southerners should cultivate a sense of humor and learn to laugh at themselves. She feels today that additional blood and irony would go far toward bringing about a solution of the South's problems.

"There are three chief dangers which the South faces at the present time," she says. "The first and most important danger is that Southern labor will be exploited in the interest of Northern capital. The low wages and long hours which obtain in many Southern industrial plants are absolutely indefensible, and the habit our chambers of commerce have of boasting about the lowness of wages is deplorable. The second danger is that we will make in the South a mad industrialism and that in so doing we will sacrifice the charm and the freedom of living. The third is that the South will surrender its intellectual attitude to the Fundamentalist point of view."

An ardent apostle of freedom of thought and action, Miss Glasgow is alarmed by the tendency on the part of present-day Southerners to use their freedom for the creation of ugliness rather than beauty.

"The South," she says, "is making the mistake of trying to create a culture and to leave out the aesthetic sense. It is impossible to build a great culture without a sense of beauty. I have just motored 1,200 miles through Virginia and am more convinced than ever that the present civilization being created in the South is the ugliest in the history of man. Mile after mile of concrete roads lined with billboards and shaded by telegraph poles! Thousands upon thousands of cars speeding to nowhere!

"There seems to be a superstition in the South that it is impossible to have good roads and to have trees at the same time. In New England and in various countries of Europe they have just as good, if not better, roads, and the trees arch overhead."

In addition to submerging its sense of beauty, Miss Glasgow feels that the modern South is dangerously near capitulation to the Fundamentalists. "We should never bargain with the forces of ignorance," she declares, her eyes flashing. Such manifestations of the South's inquisitorial spirit as anti-evolution bills and anti-Catholic crusades lead her to the conclusion that many citizens in this section of the Union are using their freedom mainly with a view to restricting the freedom of others. In this connection she says concerning prohibition:

"The thing which interests me especially is not whether we are to have prohibition, but whether we are to have humanity and mercy. Prohibition is on the side of cruelty and intolerance. A great historian has said that humanity continues to substitute one evil for another and to call it progress. In the South we are substituting murder for a mint julep and calling it progress. Prohibition is responsible for a vast deal of sham and pretense. The only art which has reached its peak in the South, or in any part of America, for that matter, is the art of hypocrisy."

Miss Glasgow looks with a wistful eye upon certain aspects of life in the Old South, notably the ability of its leaders to live and let live. But certain it is that the fine art of living attains in her its highest expression. From her delightful home she dispenses the kind of gracious hospitality which flourished in Richmond a century ago. There in the great square, high-ceilinged rooms, hung with ancestral portraits and quaint engravings and furnished with old pieces of Sheraton, Chippendale, and Heppelwhite, she entertains her friends in the grand manner.

A vivacious and clever conversationalist, she is equally at ease in discussing the historical theses of Buckle, the philosophical concepts of Berkeley, or the fiction of Julia Peterkin and Stark Young. Comely to look upon, with a graceful figure, sparkling brown eyes, slim ankles, and the complexion of a debutante, Miss Glasgow's appearance belies her years.

Her diversions, in addition to reading, include travel and golf. She concluded about fifteen years ago that horseback riding had been ruined by the advent of the automobile, and so gave it up. Usually she spends a good many of her leisure hours on the links of the Hermitage Country Club at Richmond, but a severe illness of her favorite dog, a pedigreed Sealyham, which was forced to undergo a serious operation, has prevented her from playing as often in late months as she had done previously. She confesses that she generally lands in the sixties on the nine-hole Hermitage course, but she once hung up a score of fifty-one, which is much better than average for feminine golfers.

In addition to occupying herself with golf and other forms of recreation, Miss Glasgow devotes part of her time to the work of the Virginia Society for the Prevention of Cruelty to Animals, of which she has been president for the last five years. "Animals and trees receive so little kindness and attention that I have always been especially interested in them," she explains.

Her particular affection for the canine family is evidenced not only by her attachment to "Jeremy," her Sealyham, and "Billie," her French poodle, but also by the fact that she has a remarkable collection of fifty-one porcelain dogs of different varieties, most of which she obtained in England in recent years and one of which, a Crown Derby pointer, dates back to 1780. Another is the smallest porcelain dog ever made.

Such are Miss Glasgow's principal interests. She abhors the "movies" and has been to them only three times in her life. The first was *The Birth of a Nation*, which she enjoyed because of the pictorial effects.

Someone then prevailed on her to see the screen version of *Oliver Twist* on the plea that it was a picture of surpassing excellence. She went, and vowed never again to darken the door of a "movie" palace.

"The book was so horribly distorted," she says, "that I didn't get over it for weeks." Last spring she was clamorously informed that she should by all means see Douglas Fairbanks in *The Man in the Iron Mask*. She protested, but was assured that it was a film of such sterling merit that it would undoubtedly make her a convert to the screen. So she finally consented to go. The result is best described in her own words:

"The picture had no relation whatever to Dumas or to history and was an utter falsification from beginning to end. I can imagine nothing more demoralizing than such performances. Why can't the 'movies' be made a little more intelligent?"

Like her close friend, James Branch Cabell, Richmond's other novelist of international repute, Miss Glasgow was reared in the Episcopal Church, but she no longer devotes any of her time to its rites. While this is equally true of Mr. Cabell, he lists himself in *Who's Who* as an Episcopalian, whereas Miss Glasgow lists no religious affiliation for herself.

The fact that Mr. Cabell continues to refer to himself as a churchman impresses her as amusing in the extreme. "I have often told James," she said recently, "that the funniest thing he ever wrote was the word 'Episcopalian' in *Who's Who*."

And, like Mr. Cabell again, she sees a bright future for Southern letters, now that so many Southern writers have broken the shackles which bound them to the past. Not only are there a number of these authors whose work she regards as unusually significant, but she sees in the excellence of *The Virginia Quarterly*

Review another encouraging sign of the literary *risorgimento* below the Potomac.

"It is entirely possible," she declares, "that the best writing in the United States will now be done in the South."

Certainly if this writing meets the standard of unflinching courage, scintillating wit, and exquisite craftsmanship which she herself has set, her prophecy will be fulfilled in the not distant future.

A Remedy for Virginia's Business Slump

(1931)

Like the piece on George Washington's boozing gardener, this one was a not-wholly-facetious effort to support attempts to end the disastrous Noble Experiment of the 1920s and early 1930s and secure repeal of the Volstead Act.

Down here in Virginia where corn whiskey is the almost universal drink of those whose habits have not changed since booze was outlawed, as well as of that great army of women and young people who have taken to guzzling during the decade that this has been a dry nation—down here, I say, where corn is the almost universal tipple, and is readily obtainable on short notice, it is perhaps not generally realized that this product is virtually nonexistent in certain other sections of the republic. In such benighted states as, say, New York, New Jersey or Massachusetts, it is said to be almost impossible to get a drink of honest corn despite the fact that these commonwealths abound in alcoholic spirits of many varieties.

It is true that one or two of Richmond's most progressive bootleggers are reported to have taken steps of late to remedy this situation. These enterprising citizens, interested in the further development of Virginia's industries, and perhaps moved by motives of idealism as well, have opened branch offices in Gotham, and are now engaged in providing the rum-soaked and beer-drinking citizens of that metropolis with pure mountain dew from these fastnesses off the Blue Ridge.

From the *Richmond Times-Dispatch*, March 1, 1931.

It is entirely possible that the excellent quality of the merchandise which these bootleggers are vending in the North will create such a demand in that region for Mountain Moonshine from the Mother of States that other counties will be led to emulate the great County of Franklin, 99 percent of whose population was recently reported by the Wickersham commission to be connected in one way or another with the manufacture or distribution of white mule.

It will hardly be denied that the discovery of new markets for one of Virginia's leading products will aid in the current industrial development of the state, and stimulate business in its now depressed condition. At the same time, the substitution of good Virginia corn for the hair tonic and shellac which is being swigged in New York and other cities to the north should mean much to the health of the citizenry of those communities. Some of the beverages which are now being consumed there play havoc with the lining of one's esophagus, and the substitution of moonshine would prove a genuine benefaction to the suffering population.

Indeed I am informed by an excellent authority on such matters, a man who has tasted many brews and observed their effects upon the human system, that corn juice such as is currently manufactured in the hollows and coves of the Virginia mountains is the most salubrious of all distilled beverages. This connoisseur is emphatic in the belief that corn is superior in purity to any other variety of booze, and that such backward regions as New England and New York should abandon their scalp lotions and furniture polish and learn to appreciate the many good qualities of Virginia moonshine.

Of course some good whiskey is drunk in the territory referred to. A good deal of red liquor is smuggled in from Canada, Cuba, the Bahamas, Europe, etc., but much of this is diluted. Even when it isn't it is frequently inferior to pure corn, insofar as its healthfulness is concerned.

Here is an idea for our boosters to get busy with. Smithfield hams, Albemarle pippins, and other Virginia products have been widely marketed and are known in foreign lands, but as yet Virginia corn has not been put over to the outlanders in a big way. We have heard a good deal in recent years of the Old Dominion's undeveloped resources. This seems to be the biggest of them all. If somebody will take hold of it and put it across, the business slump can be brought to an end, at least in Virginia, and the resultant prosperity diffused to all other elements of the population. It is even possible that the average citizen will then receive an income at least approaching that of a prohibition agent.

What would be the state's principal markets, in the event that its whiskey industry was developed to the full extent of its possibilities? Reference already has been made to New York and New England which as yet have not become acquainted with the Virginia brand of wet goods. This thirsty section of the republic would probably consume the output of several counties, all of them operating full speed ahead as Franklin is now doing. In such an event, there would certainly be no further unemployment problem in those counties. The entire populace could heave to and unite in the manufacture of mountain dew with which to moisten the parched throats of Bostonians and New Yorkers.

Since the other Southern states all make large quantities of moonshine, just as the Old Dominion does, there would be little or no market for the Virginia brand in Dixie, at one and the same time the chief producer of corn whiskey and of votes for prohibition.

Thus with the South eliminated as a market, enterprising promoters of the Virginia corn whiskey industry would have to turn to fresh fields and pastures new. In addition to the entire northeastern seaboard, in itself a huge and populous area, gratifying sales could be made in the states fronting on the Great Lakes. True, they get a lot of stuff from Canada now, but with a concentrated campaign in the area, handled by gifted young men who know the principles of modern merchandising, the sales resistance of this region could probably be broken down. Virginia's message could be put across with a wallop in newspapers and magazines, just as the makers of high-class champagne are now ballyhooing their goods in the advertising columns of the *New Yorker*, and Mabel Willebrandt's outfit which sells unfermented fruit juice is marketing it on a national scale, with instructions on what to do and how to do it.

Indeed, it might be worthwhile for the sponsors of the Virginia project to consider asking Mrs. Willebrandt to serve as an attorney for them. That great prohibitionist states that it is only because of her love for the dry cause that she is interested in selling unfermented fruit juices to the American people. It ought to be possible to persuade her that the cause would be further aided if drinkers of hair tonic could be persuaded to relinquish it for so sound a beverage as Virginia mountain dew. This view might even prevail with the Anti-Saloon League, if Mabel presented it to them in judicious fashion, for she was reported in the press to have been loudly applauded by the leaguers who heard her explain "in camera" why the sale of her fruit juices would be of inestimable benefit to the cause of morality.

A large section of the Middle West would, alas, be eliminated as a market for Virginia's product, since that is where the corn grows tallest. It is but natural that the citizenry of this dry section of the United States should be extensively engaged in converting grain into booze. But on the Pacific Coast it is said that corn juice is hard to find. Consequently Virginia should have a market in California, the home state of President Hoover, whose present position on prohibition is unknown to the public, since he has had nothing to say on the subject for a couple of weeks.

From coast to coast, then, the Old Dominion should at once inaugurate a selling program designed to tell the world about Virginia corn. Even without the aid of Madame Willebrandt and the Anti-Saloon League the campaign can be made a success, but if the co-operation of the moral and religious forces can be enlisted it will be so much the better. A snappy slogan should be devised, something on the order of "Stop Gnawing the Varnish Off the Furniture and Try Our Moonshine from Contented Moonshiners" or "Swear Off Shellac for Virginia Mountain Dew: Packs a Kick Like a Missouri Mule, but Not a Hangover in a Hogshead." Soothing messages of this nature could be crooned over the radio by Rudy Vallee or boop-boop-a-dooped by Helen Kane, and a concentrated campaign of advertising launched on a national scale. In no time the orders would begin pouring in, and Virginia's unemployment problem would be solved. If the authorities fail to take advantage of this statesmanlike suggestion they have no one but themselves to blame.

1932: The Confederates Return
(1984)

In 1932 Richmond was preparing in all possible ways for the coming of the Confederate veterans. Douglas Southall Freeman, editor of the *Richmond News Leader*, already recognized as a leading authority on the Civil War although his masterly books on the subject lay in the future, hailed the approaching gathering. Under the caption *They Are Coming Again!* he editorialized: "Nothing like next week's reunion has ever been held in America. Nothing like it can ever be held again."

The convention's general chairman was Robert T. Barton, Jr., a prominent young lawyer whose family had a stunning record in the Civil War. His father fought in the famous Stonewall Brigade, and three of his uncles were killed in the war. Another uncle, Major Randolph Barton, was wounded five times and had seven horses shot from under him. He lived to become a leading attorney in Baltimore. Robert Barton, Jr., a captain of field artillery in World War I, would serve as a colonel in World War II. His assistant chairmen were G. Jeter Jones, Henry S. Hotchkiss, and Lee O. Miller.

It was taken for granted that there would be ailing veterans at the conclave, and instructions for their care were issued by Dr. Robert C. Bryan, chairman of the medical committee. He pointed out that men averaging in age from eighty-five to ninety "require the greatest care and attention," and urged that, in the event of any accident or illness, Memorial Hospital be called for an ambulance. The public was also asked to invite into their

From *The Last Review, Richmond, 1932* (Chapel Hill, N.C.: Algonquin Books of Chapel Hill, 1984).

homes any veteran who needed to lie down or who wanted a drink of water or anything else.

"Please remember," Dr. Bryan went on, "that these old men know much better than you what they have been accustomed to eat, and the routine of their lives. Let them have what they want. Eighty-five years of habit cannot be changed in twenty-four hours." Addressing the housewives of Richmond, Dr. Bryan opined: "You are probably a good housekeeper and excellent hostess, but you are not a doctor. . . . You must remember that the heat, advanced age, excitement of travel, irregular habits, and the reunion work a great hardship on these frail bodies."

The Soldiers' Home hospital was upgraded for the occasion, with medical men in charge during the day and trained nurses on duty. There appears to have been no abnormal number of serious illnesses in the ranks of the vets, and only the usual minor afflictions.

The special events in Richmond began on Monday, June 20, when General C. A. De Saussure of Nashville, commander-in-chief of the United Confederate Veterans, arrived with his entourage to a salute of seventeen guns. The Richmond Light Infantry Blues was his local escort. This salute was followed by the raising of the Confederate flag over the Capitol. Several bands gave a concert that evening at Camp De Saussure, the special designation given Lee Camp Soldiers' Home in Richmond's West End, where many of the visiting veterans were quartered.

Lee Camp No. 1, UCV, had been organized in 1883 at Richmond to care for needy veterans. A site for a Soldiers' Home at the intersection of Grove Road, later known as Grove Avenue, and what was later termed the Boulevard was acquired the next year. The home opened January 1, 1885. As a starter an old building was renovated, and other structures were acquired gradually. When completed the home included cottages, a dining hall, a hospital, and a chapel. Cottages were donated by various individuals; the state of Virginia appropriated $35,000; and the city of Richmond raised $5,000 for the chapel. From the chapel, a modest frame structure still standing in 1983, some seventeen hundred veterans were buried. All but two of the buildings were torn down after the last inmate died in 1941. The Virginia Museum of Fine Arts occupies the site. The Richmond home, one of fifteen scattered over the South, was the best known.

The GAR post in Newark, New Jersey, was the first of all the contributors to the home; it sent one hundred dollars in gold in the early 1880s. Shortly thereafter General U. S. Grant sent his check for five hundred dollars. He was invited in 1884 to attend a fair to raise money for the institution but found it impossible. The former commander of the armies of the Union wrote, wishing success to the committee in charge in its effort to erect "for all brave men who need it a home and rest from cares." And he went on to say: "The men who faced each other in deadly combat can well afford to be the best of friends now, and only strive for rivalry in seeing which can be the best citizens of the grandest country on earth."

When General Grant died in 1885, both Richmond and Virginia showed their admiration for the man who had demonstrated such magnanimity. Governor William E. Cameron and four companies of Virginia militia attended the obsequies in New York, while the Virginia State Democratic Convention passed resolutions of sorrow. In Richmond business was suspended throughout the day of the funeral, and flags were flown at half-mast. The Richmond Howitzers fired a salute.

In 1932 many of the veterans had stopped over in Petersburg en route to Richmond to witness the dedication of the Petersburg National Military Park. The program included a pageant with seven scenes, among them the Battle of the Crater and the battle of June 9, 1864, when the city was saved from a surprise attack by the bravery of a citizen force. This latter feat is commemorated on a tablet in historic Blandford Church, which tells of "the Citizen Soldiers of Petersburg, the gray-haired sires and beardless youths who . . . laid down their lives near this venerable church in successful defense of our altars and firesides."

Richmond opened its heart to the men who had fought for the South from 1861 to 1865. "Everything is Free," the convention program proclaimed, and the city's ordinary citizens, as well as its leaders, put forth all possible efforts to make the visitors welcome and at home. They in turn gave many evidences that they were enjoying themselves.

This reunion was not an occasion for stirring up intersectional animosities and opening old wounds. Although there were instances when lingering antagonism against the North was shown on specific issues by aged individuals, for the most part it was a good-natured gathering held in a relaxed atmosphere. Hospitality was lavish and virtually unlimited, although this was the bottom of the Great Depression.

Striking evidence of intersectional amity was seen in the presence of two especially honored guests. They were Dr. George Bolling Lee, the only surviving grandson of General R. E. Lee, and Lieutenant Colonel Ulysses S. Grant III, grandson of General U. S. Grant. Dr. Lee and Colonel Grant got along famously and were photographed shaking hands most cordially.

Confederate flags lined Broad Street, decorated the statues of Confederate heroes, and hung from homes. The flag of the Confederacy flew from the Capitol throughout the convention, but it was not the same banner that fluttered there when Richmond fell on April 3, 1865. That flag, hauled down and carried off by a Union officer, was graciously returned in 1927; but it was too fragile to be flown during the reunion. It had been made while the Civil War was in progress, at the request of Virginia's Governor "Extra Billy" Smith, who asked the Misses Sallie and Margaret Munford to fashion a new flag to replace the tattered Confederate oriflamme atop the Capitol. They did so, and by a remarkable set of circumstances Miss Sallie Munford was present more than six decades later at the ceremony in Richmond for the flag's return. She was then Mrs. Charles H. Talbott, and she readily identified the flag as the one that she and her sister had stitched in their Franklin Street home at the height of the Civil War.

Veterans attending the 1932 reunion were among the visitors to

Capitol Square, where the Confederate banner flew. I saw them sitting on the benches feeding peanuts to the squirrels. The peaceful scene was in glaring contrast to that of April 3, 1865, when after the few remaining Confederate forces had left the city, the area immediately south of the Square became a roaring inferno, and the Square itself was filled with terrified women and children. The fire had been set in tobacco warehouses by Confederate officials, in an effort to prevent the tobacco from falling into Union hands, but a high wind sprang up and spread the flames. Every effort was made by the Union troops to control the conflagration when they took over the city, but Richmond's business district was virtually wiped out.

At 6 P.M. each day a sunset gun was fired from Capitol Hill and at 8 P.M. there was special entertainment at Camp De Saussure. It included musical numbers, dancing of the minuet and Virginia Reel by local high-school pupils, Old Time Fiddlers, the Sabbath Glee Club of Negro singers, Blackface Artists, a number called "Hack and Sack," and other skits. A similar program was offered on the next two nights.

Before these programs began, space was left in the schedule of events for "Amos 'n' Andy," the radio program that achieved almost unprecedented popularity and ran uninterruptedly for thirty-two years. "Amos 'n' Andy" was such a universal favorite that it was listed specifically for 6 P.M. daily on the UCV's convention program, so that no competing event would interfere with the veterans' slapping their knees and guffawing at the humorous sallies—along with some forty million other Americans. Many of the delegates would undoubtedly have felt deprived if this opportunity had not been offered. Motion-picture houses in that era actually interrupted their programs and piped in the complete dialogue of "Amos 'n' Andy" for fifteen minutes, after which the showing of the film resumed. The two principal characters were played by Freeman Gosden and Charles Correll, white men who impersonated blacks. Other "blacks" were Kingfish, Lightnin', Madame Queen, and Brother Crawford. For decades their antics were regarded as inoffensive, but as the civil rights movement gathered momentum in the 1950s they came to be considered objectionable, and the show finally went off the air. The old vets relished it immensely in 1932.

On the opening day of the convention I was sent out to the Old Soldiers' Home by the *Times-Dispatch* to report on the state of affairs among the newly arrived delegates. They were getting acquainted, and swapping stories of the war, some of which were of decidedly dubious authenticity. The federal government had furnished, without charge, enough army cots to care for two thousand men, together with sheets, blankets, pillows, and pillowcases. About 750 visiting veterans were staying at Camp De Saussure, with some 650 more at Camp Robert E. Lee in Robert E. Lee School, and 100 at Camp Father Ryan in Benedictine School.

"There was nothing of rancor in their good-natured reminiscences," I wrote. "Gone was the ancient animosity for the 'Yanks.' They talked of the war as though all the delirium of the sixties had been obliterated by the flood of years. . . .

"They sat under the trees or on the cottage porches, talking of the days of long ago, when 'Marse Robert' led them to victory, and the shell-torn banners of the Confederacy perched for one triumphant moment on the heights of Seminary Ridge, only to be withdrawn when reinforcements failed to come up."

Unfortunately I had the shell-torn banners of the Confederacy perching at the wrong place at Gettysburg. It was Cemetery, not Seminary, Ridge which marked the high tide of Pickett's immortal charge. Seminary Ridge was the height from which Lee surveyed the sanguinary scene.

The benches under the trees at the Soldiers' Home were an admirable locale for the recounting of one's heroic exploits during the war or deeds of derring-do attributable to others. A typical stretcher was the yarn related by one hardened warrior, reputedly from the state of South Carolina. "When we was blowed up at the Crater," said he, "me and my men was th'owed up in the air. As we went up, we met our captain a-comin' down, and as he went by he hollered, 'Rally boys when you hit the ground!'"

Breakfast was served for the visiting delegates at Camp De Saussure from 6 A.M. to 9 A.M. Apparently it was theorized that at least a few of the old boys were accustomed to rising early and breakfasting betimes. For those of a somewhat more somnolent disposition there was reveille at 7 A.M. to the rousing notes of one of several bands. The musical organizations that played for these and other functions during the convention were the Mississippi State Teachers' College Band; the Augusta, Georgia, Police Band; the Little Rock, Arkansas, High School Band; the Charlottesville, Virginia, Municipal Band; and the Clarksville, Virginia, Boys' and Girls' Band.

At least once a day, and usually twice, there was an illustrated lecture in the Soldiers' Home Chapel on Generals Robert E. Lee and Stonewall Jackson, "courtesy of Mrs. Lottie K. Browne."

All the Richmond hotels were jammed with visitors—not only members of the UCV but also those of the Sons of Confederate Veterans and the Confederated Southern Memorial Association, which were holding conventions in the city. Many were guests in private homes. Others were in various lodgings arranged in schools and colleges.

The prohibition law was still in full force in Richmond and everywhere else in 1932. Repeal did not come until the next year. Although there was no open violation of the law during the convention, insofar as I was aware, it may be safely assumed that prohibition was no more effective at that time than at any other. Hospitality around the flowing bowl was entirely unofficial, but in private homes and elsewhere one may take it for granted that successful efforts were made to assuage the thirst of the visitors. The two Richmond newspapers, the *Times-Dispatch* and *News Leader*, were both vigorously opposed to the dry law as being completely unenforceable and objectionable on other grounds as well. They recorded the confiscation and destruction on the city dump of liquor seized during the convention. Whether this raid had any relation to the presence of the Confederates was not made known. Another amusing episode occurred when nine bottles of confiscated home brew blew up in police court, furnishing an obligato to the music of the convention bands outside.

The local papers gave lavish coverage to the convention, with hundreds of pictures and many columns of type, although they by no means matched the amount of space devoted to the reunions of 1890 and 1907. Much space also was devoted to the Democratic national convention, which was meeting in Chicago to nominate a candidate for president of the United States. Franklin D. Roosevelt was making his successful bid for the nomination, and there was a short-lived presidential boom for ex-Governor Harry F. Byrd of Virginia.

During the UCV convention the Richmond newspapers adopted the practice of identifying each of its writers by a forebear who served in the Confederate forces. My contributions were accordingly signed "By Virginius Dabney, grandson of Captain Virginius Dabney, CSA, of General John B. Gordon's staff."

After my initial trip I went out to the Old Soldiers' Home again, in order to interview one or more of the half-dozen Negro body servants who were attending the convention. There I found Uncle Bill Wilson, who boasted of his prowess in purloining chickens, pigs, corn, and watermelons for his master. On one of these foraging expeditions he encountered a Yankee bushwhacker, who fired on him. Uncle Bill's horse bolted and slammed into a tree, banging up Bill's knee so badly that he had been a cripple ever since—for some seventy years. "Yas, suh, I'se crippled," he said sadly, "and I reckon I always will be"—an assumption that appeared hardly susceptible of contradiction.

But the most celebrated of the black servants was undoubtedly Uncle Steve Eberhardt, whose prowess as a raider of hen roosts was proverbial. He attended all UCV reunions over many years, with chicken feathers protruding from his hat and clothing. Captain James Dinkins wrote in the *Confederate Veteran* of his appearance and actions in Richmond. Uncle Steve was invited to the platform at the Mosque, where the convention sessions were being held, Dinkins said. He was a member of the 10th Georgia, and he wanted to speak. "His hat and his pockets were full of chicken feathers," Dinkins wrote. Steve stated: "I am a hundred and seven years old, I have always been a white man's nigger, and the Yankees can't change me, suh!" He drew loud applause.

Obviously a relic of a bygone era, Uncle Steve appears in Bell I. Wiley's *Southern Negroes: 1861–1865*. Wiley wrote that "the bosom of his 'Confederate Gray' overcoat was almost completely covered with reunion badges." Flaunting the tail-feathers of his pilfered fowls, the aged black proclaimed himself "the biggest chicken-thief in the Confederacy."

These Negro body servants sat under the trees at the Soldiers' Home with the white veterans. Many of both groups were smoking their pipes or chewing their plugs. There were emotional moments, as when one of the white Confederates was asked which general he served under in the war. "Jackson, sir," came the proud reply, as tears welled in the old man's eyes.

Captain Dinkins wrote that the convention was attended mainly by "generals," and that no more than fifty nongenerals were on hand for any of the official sessions. He himself appeared on the program as Major General Dinkins. "There were a great many generals," said he. "I doubt if Caesar had as many generals in his big army when he crossed the Rubicon as there were in Richmond." These UCV generals had been officers of lower rank, even privates, during the war; the actual generals were all dead. On the evening program of Wednesday, June 22, there were no fewer than twelve generals either making speeches or introducing speakers. The convention was called to order by General William McK. Evans, commander of the Virginia Division, UCV. He presented General W. B. Freeman, honorary commander for life, and father of Douglas Freeman. Another notable participant in the program was the Rev. Giles B. Cooke, honorary chaplain-general for life and the last surviving member of General Robert E. Lee's staff.

A significant relic on view during the conclave was the tremendous sword of Heros von Borcke, the Prussian dragoon who crossed the Atlantic and ran the blockade to fight for the Confederacy. Von Borcke, who became General J. E. B. Stuart's adjutant-general, had knelt by Stuart's bed, his huge frame wracked with sobs, as the great cavalryman's life ebbed away following his mortal wound at Yellow Tavern.

Also to be seen during the convention was "an original John Brown pike," wielded by Brown or one of his men in their attempt at Harper's Ferry to incite a slave insurrection on the eve of the war, an ill-starred effort that ended, for Brown, on the gallows. But while the fanatic Brown forfeited his life, his soul "went marching on." Stephen Vincent Benét, in his memorable poem *John Brown's Body*, speaks of Brown's "singing bones" and the inspiration they gave to the antislavery forces of the North. "The Battle Hymn of the Republic" and the song "John Brown's Body" were sung by the Union Army's marching thousands; and the war became, in the minds of many, a great antislavery crusade. Brown himself wrote that he was "worth inconceivably more to *hang* than for any other purpose."

Senator Tom Connally of Texas spoke in stentorian tones at the opening of the Sons of Confederate Veterans convention in the Mosque. Scorning the microphone, considered absolutely essential by virtually all speakers in the huge hall, the orator from the Lone Star State shook the rafters as he addressed a packed house.

"I do not like the words 'Lost Cause,'" the speaker boomed. "The example set by Southern women during the war can never be called lost. Nor is Jackson's military skill lost to military students, nor the towering military leadership of Lee." Connally decried the statements of some critics that the South fought "to keep the slaves," saying that the vast majority of the men who fought never owned a slave and never expected to own one.

Senator Connally also spoke at the dedication of the handsome new building of the Home for Confederate Women, adjoining the Old Soldiers' Home. The widows of Confederate soldiers had been housed for many years in an extremely modest house on Grace Street. Most of them had died by 1932, when the well-appointed new residence was opened. Now, as the number of widows dwindled, daughters of the men who fought for the Confederacy were placed in the institution. A half-century later, in 1983, there were no widows and thirty daughters in a building that accommodates seventy-nine.

Dedication of the Richmond Battlefield Parks, comprising the blood-soaked fields around the city over which the Confederate and Union armies fought, was a feature of the reunion program. Five hundred acres were included in the total parks area, and the ceremony was held in a grove at Frayser's Farm, scene of one of the desperate encounters of the Seven Days. Battlefields included in the park system, which was ceded to the state, were those of Seven Pines, Mechanicsville, Gaines' Mill, Savage Station, Frayser's Farm, Malvern Hill, Bethesda Church, Cold Harbor, and Fort Harrison.

Douglas Southall Freeman and J. Ambler Johnston, a prominent Richmond engineer, were primarily responsible for the creation of this park system. Johnston, like Freeman, was a great authority on these battlefields. He arranged the program of dedication, and Freeman took part in it. Tazewell M. Carrington, president of the Richmond Battlefield Parks Corporation, presided and formally presented the park area to the commonwealth. Lieutenant Governor James H. Price accepted it. Governor John Garland Pollard appeared on several other programs during the convention but not this one.

Major General Lytle Brown, chief of engineers, U.S. Army, was the principal speaker. The affair took an unexpected turn when Douglas Freeman sought to introduce him. The Confederate veterans in the audience decided that they wanted to get into the act. As Freeman began discussing some of the events that had occurred on this historic ground, veterans began interrupting with a wide-ranging list of questions. "The veterans insisted that he go on and name all Confederate officers through the rank of colonel, all brigades, all divisions and all major battles," A. Judson Evans of the *Times-Dispatch* wrote facetiously, with obvious exaggeration.

"What about Joe Wheeler?" one Confederate wanted to know. "Have you ever heard of the Rockbridge Artillery?" said another. "I was present when Stonewall was shot; what about him?" a third interjected. "Ever hear of Pickett?"; "What about the navy?"; and so on. Freeman answered them all, but still another wanted to be heard. "You know about the Crater? Right over there in Petersburg—five hundred South Carolinians blowed up in one night, and you ain't mentioned it!"

Dr. Freeman finally managed to introduce General Brown.

A notable event on the next day was the presentation at the Confederate Museum of the anchor of the *Virginia-Merrimac* to the Confederate Memorial Literary Society, which operates the museum. Miss Mary Maury Fitzgerald, granddaughter of Commodore Matthew Fontaine Maury, made the presentation. Miss Sally Archer Anderson, president of the Confederate Memorial Literary Society, accepted the anchor for that organization. It was placed in the yard of the museum, where it can be seen today.

A bronze marker commemorating the inauguration of Jefferson Davis as Confederate president was dedicated at the Washington Monument in Capitol Square. The Davis inauguration had taken place in a pouring rain on February 22, 1862, with the crowd shivering under umbrellas. The speaker for the unveiling of the tablet seventy years later was Rosewell Page, brother of Thomas Nelson Page, and a state official. He read from his ambitious poem *The Iliads of the South*, a long series of verses occupying 26 "books" and 190 printed pages. The writing of poetry was hardly Mr. Page's forte. His lines on Jefferson Davis are typical of the whole:

> With Jefferson Davis, a State's Rights man,
> Provisional President, ere last four joined;
> Elected after Constitution framed,
> By all the States of the Confederacy.
> Experienced and eloquent in speech,
> Belonging to the ancient State's Rights school,
> And ever firmly set in his own ways.
> Right gallantly, he fought in Mexico;
> His statesmanship he learned from great Calhoun;
> In halls of Congress well he bore himself
> As Mississippi's leading senator:
> The Secretary of War he once had been;
> And popular when Pierce was President.
> In casemate manacled a martyr made,
> Vicarious sufferer for the South,
> He soon became; and has been since so deemed!

> Afraid to test Secession in the courts
> Lest it be legally by courts upheld,
> His foes dismissed the treasonable charge
> When Charles O'Connor [*sic*] and the rest appeared,
> And Horace Greeley joined in his bail bond!

The elderly warriors at the UCV convention did some high stepping at the grand ball the night of July 23 in the Grays' Armory. As Mary Binford Hobson wrote in the *Times-Dispatch*: "Spry and gallant as they were back in the days when their partners wore hoop skirts and pantaloons, these happy gentlemen swung their partners gaily along the Grand March, did some fancy jigging to the music of the old time fiddlers, and interrupted the square dancing to kiss the hands of the cheering spectators, or to chuck some of the pretty girls under the chin." There was life in the old boys yet.

The SCV held its grand ball at the armory the next night. An elaborate figure devised by Dr. William R. Dancey of Savannah, incoming commander-in-chief, took an hour and a half to run off, so intricate were the maneuvers. As usual the playing of "Dixie" elicited a storm of applause and shouts. Those were the days when the rousing Confederate song could be played without inhibitions.

The National Broadcasting Company came up with the idea of interviewing some of the old Confederates on the radio. The aged warriors entered into the activity with spirit—so much so, according to Joseph Bryan III, the Richmond author, that the show had to be cut short midway during one interview.

Bryan, whose grandfather, Joseph Bryan, served gallantly during the war as one of John S. Mosby's famous partisans, reports that the radio program began with a rendition of the Rebel yell by a group of a dozen veterans. Age had made their voices weak and thin, and one of the old gentlemen sought to compensate by giving so tremendous an effort that his suspenders snapped and his pants fell down.

Wade Arnold, handling the program for NBC, then opened an interview with "Uncle Charlie," a nonagenarian from New Orleans, last name unknown. Uncle Charlie reported that the uniform he was wearing had been made for him by his "Maw" when he enlisted and "jined Gen'l Beaurehgyahd."

Arnold sought to pursue the story of the uniform, but Uncle Charlie had other ideas. "Nemmine *mah* close," he said. "Ah'll tell you-all sump'n 'bout *women's* close!"

The script did not call for discourse on that subject, and Arnold attempted to get his guest back on track, but Uncle Charlie would have none of it. "They's a scandal, that's what!" he continued. "Ah mean short skirts!"

Again the announcer moved to change the topic without success. "No matter wheh you go," continued Uncle Charlie. "—on the street, in the theayter, in the sportin' house . . ."

That did it. An on-the-air reference to a "sportin' house" was, in that era, scandalous beyond the pale. The interview was abruptly terminated.

The grand parade of the Confederate veterans, the last in history, passed along Richmond streets on Friday, June 24, as the Stars and Bars and other flags of the Confederacy fluttered from windows and were waved from sidewalks. There were lumps in many throats, including mine, as the procession passed, for it was realized by all that this scene could never be repeated. The aged participants who had served under Beauregard at Shiloh or charged Union breastworks with Hood had to make the trip in automobiles since they were no longer able to go on foot. A group of veterans waved a sign calling for repeal of the Eighteenth Amendment, which brought laughter and cheers.

The numerous bands played Southern airs, with "Dixie" the most popular of all. Members of the Richmond Light Infantry Blues, a historic military unit going back for its origins to 1789, were dashingly impressive in their Napoleonic dress uniforms, refurbished with new facing and shakos. They were led by Major Mills F. Neal, their longtime commander. Also in the parade were the Richmond Grays and the Howitzers with their horses and field pieces. Officials of the SCV, UDC, and CSMA occupied prominent places in the line. Other patriotic groups were there, including the 40-and-8 of World War I days. There was applause for all marching units.

The Confederate veterans blew kisses to the ladies and smiled at the children as the procession passed. An especially lively participant was Major John Crowley, a Louisiana Tiger who had served during the war as a rider to carry secret dispatches for President Jefferson Davis. Holding tightly to the banner of the South, he insisted on riding part of the time astride the hood of the car in which Virginia's adjutant-general, S. Gardner Waller, was traveling. But when the parade passed the statues on Monument Avenue, Major Crowley dismounted and saluted to each one. "Ten thousand men like that could lick any army in the world," said General Waller. The major was deemed "a gallant figure by all," the newspaper account declared.

While in the city for the reunion the aged veterans were well looked after by the local citizenry. Richmond's young ladies in particular delighted in bestowing attention upon the old soldiers. Indeed, so smitten by the charms of one such hostess was a veteran from Tennessee that after returning home he wrote requesting a photograph of the lady, and upon receiving it, proposed matrimony:

I feel as if the Lord had something to do with our meeting. When I met you you seemed to be the one I have been looking for. I feel that we could get along fine and my lawyer is working to get my pension now. Write quick. I want to know what you think of being Mrs. I—— instead of Miss C——. There was a woman in Biloxi Miss met a man, talked and then they were married in the parade.

Write and tell me when and where the next reunion will be, as I never hear anything like that, and I want to meet you there, if not before.

Answer quick and a long letter, and be sure and tell me how it will suit you to have your name changed. You have worn the C—— name long enough.

Give your mother my warm regards.

Your true Friend
J. A. I——

P.S. If you get letters from any one concerning mine and your case pay no attention to it.

The young lady in question, though flattered, wrote back that she was not ready to consider matrimony just yet.

One of the last acts of the forty-second annual reunion of UCV was to elect General Homer T. Atkinson of Petersburg commander-in-chief, succeeding General De Saussure. General Atkinson was the last survivor of the gallant group of old men and boys who had saved Petersburg in the battle of June 9, 1864. He was only fifteen at the time. Subsequently he managed to join the army, apparently by giving his age as seventeen. In 1865 he was commissioned second lieutenant in Company B, 19th regiment of the Mississippi Infantry. Later Atkinson was captured; he refused to take the oath of allegiance and remained in prison until midsummer 1865.

Many of the delegates to the convention left for their homes on Saturday morning, June 25, as they did not feel up to the planned side trip to Washington aboard a special train. Events during the four days in Richmond had left a goodly number exhausted. The relatively hardy minority took the train to the nation's capital for a series of events, notably a parade down Pennsylvania Avenue. It was headed, spectacularly, by four veterans on horseback who had ridden with Forrest. They made a brave show. In the line as it moved past the reviewing stand, in addition to the Confederates, were several military bands, troops of cavalry, blue jackets, Marine and Coast Guard units, veterans of various wars, Boy Scouts, and even the Daughters of Job.

President Herbert Hoover's failure to review the parade was a serious disappointment. Perhaps exhausted by his trials and tribulations during the deepening depression, the president had departed for his camp on the Rapidan, and Secretary of the Navy Charles Francis Adams, Jr., did the honors. Adams was an appropriate choice, since his father, the New England historian, had been one of Robert E. Lee's staunchest defenders, saying that if he had been in Lee's place in 1861, he would have done what Lee did.

The program of events in and around Washington included a basket picnic on the field of Manassas or Bull Run, the placing of a wreath on the tomb of the Unknown Soldier at Arlington by

General De Saussure, and another on the Confederate Monument by Dr. George R. Tabor, former commander-in-chief of the Sons of Confederate Veterans. As the final event the U.S. Marine Band gave a concert.

After 1932, there would not be enough survivors of the Civil War to hold another Confederate convention that could be called a major reunion in the usual sense. A gathering billed as the final reunion of the United Confederate Veterans took place in Norfolk, Virginia, in late May and early June, 1951. Only three veterans, aged 104 and 105, out of the twelve or more who were still living, managed to attend. The meeting was held in conjunction with the convention of the Sons of Confederate Veterans, hundreds of whom were present.

The three members of UCV who came were William Joshua Bush of Fitzgerald, Georgia; William D. Townsend of Olla, Louisiana; and John Salling of Slant, Virginia. All three were "generals." General Bush, 105, was the liveliest. "I can hear good, I can see good, I can taste good, and I can kiss any damn woman who wants to be kissed," said he. His wife felt it necessary to admonish him several times: "Hush, Daddy, stop that cussing."

Richmond Starts Its Third Century
(1933)

Richmond will observe its 200th birthday next Tuesday. It was on September 19, 1733, that Colonel William Byrd II, of "Westover," the most gifted Virginian of his generation, wrote in his *A Journey to the Land of Eden*, which describes a trip he made with several companions through the wilderness for the purpose of opening iron mines:

"When we got home, we laid the foundation of two large Citys. One at Shacco's, to be called Richmond, and the other at the point of the Appamattux River, to be named Petersburgh. These Major Mayo offered to lay out into Lots without Fee or Reward. The Truth of it is, these two places being the uppermost Landing of James and Appamattux Rivers, are naturally intended for Marts, where the Traffic of the Outer Inhabitants must Center. Thus did we build not Castles only, but also Citys in the Air."

Following its establishment as a frontier trading center, Richmond gradually became more important until it superseded Williamsburg as the capital of the state in 1779. Then, in 1861, it became the capital of the Confederacy as well.

It is to this latter fact that the Richmond of today owes much of its charm. Ghosts of the leaders of the Lost Cause stalk through streets which reverberated seventy-one years ago to the echoing thunder of the Seven Days, and the phantom banners of the Gray hosts flutter in the wind. It is true that, compared with certain other Southern cities—Charleston, S.C., for example—Richmond is, on the whole, rather lacking in "atmosphere." The principal residential section is quite new, and is for the most part not

From the *New York Herald Tribune*, September 17, 1933.

unlike the residential sections in scores of other American towns. Such late eighteenth- and early nineteenth-century homes as remain are chiefly in other and older quarters. Frequently they are occupied by "poor whites" or Negroes.

But if altogether too many of these mansions have been relinquished by the families which erected them, and if others have succumbed to the devastating march of "progress," there are corners of Richmond where the Old South lives again and the atmosphere of antebellum days may be readily recreated.

One of the eighteenth-century homes which is still in an excellent state of preservation is the house once occupied by John Marshall. Some years ago a group of up-and-coming makers of municipal whoopee suggested that the Marshall House ought to be demolished. It appeared that a public school was about to be erected nearby and that the pupils would need additional room in which to play squat tag and ring-around-the-rosy during recess. The more progressive members of the populace thought this a much more important consideration than the preservation of the house in which America's greatest jurist lived for forty-five years. The plan to pull down the building was thwarted only by the determined and vigorous opposition of the town's more historically minded citizens.

The effort to save another storied structure about a decade later was less successful. This was the great, pillared Van Lew House, home of the famous Federal spy, Elizabeth Van Lew, during the Civil War. General Grant said that this woman forwarded to him the most valuable information he received from the Confederate capital during the four years of conflict. Certainly her exploits were little short of miraculous, for she was an agent of the Union in the very citadel of the Confederacy, and although she was frequently under suspicion, she managed to carry on her elaborate system of espionage unhindered.

After the war, when these activities became known, she was shunned by virtually all her fellow Virginians. Even the federal government, which had rewarded her with an appointment as postmistress of Richmond, subsequently lost interest in her. She died in 1900 with scarcely a friend in the world, and they carried her to old Shockoe Cemetery. Few Richmonders of the present generation recall her deeds or know where she lies buried. But those antiquarians who stroll occasionally among the mossy tombs in the ancient golgotha on North Second Street find her place of sepulture there, marked by a jagged rock which bears this inscription:

> Elizabeth L. Van Lew
> 1818   1900
> She risked everything that is dear to man—
> friends, fortune, comfort, health, life itself, all
> for the one absorbing desire of her heart—
> that slavery might be abolished and the Union preserved.
>
> ———
>
> This Boulder
> from the Capitol Hill in Boston is a tribute from
> Massachusetts Friends.

The air of leisure and Old Worldliness which hangs about Shockoe Cemetery and other sections of Richmond contrasts strangely with the spick and span, twentieth-century atmosphere of Monument Avenue in the West End. Progressively inclined visitors doubtless regard Monument Avenue as a greater asset to the city than all its decaying mansions and its pre-revolutionary churchyards rolled into one. It is a boulevard in the best tradition of Chicago or Kansas City, adorned with statues of Lee, Jackson, Stuart, Davis, and Maury, all Confederate heroes—a kind of Confederate *Siegesallee*, in fact, with a grass plot and trees down the center and handsome residences and apartment houses lining both sides.

When the first of the statues, that of Lee, was erected in 1890, there was vigorous opposition to the site because at that time it was a considerable distance out of town and a "mudhole" besides. But the populace turned out en masse and insisted on dragging the bronze with ropes more than half a mile to the appointed place.

Just before the Jefferson Davis monument was unveiled it is said that an urchin surreptitiously placed a lemon in the statue's outstretched palm, so that when the covering was withdrawn the president of the Confederacy seemed in the act of handing the aforesaid lemon to the large and distinguished gathering which had come to do him honor.

Once in a while on Monument Avenue a venerable inmate of the nearby Soldiers' Home is seen to stop in front of the great pedestal from which Lee, seated on Traveler, gazes out over his beloved Southland. Snapping his heels smartly together so as to jangle the bronze medals pinned to his faded gray uniform, the veteran salutes his old commander.

But if the face of Lee is turned toward the Dixie which he defended, the effigy of Jackson on the same thoroughfare looks into the eye of the foe. It is said that when the figure of the meteoric Stonewall was erected eighteen years ago his soldiers objected to his being made to turn his back on the Yankees. They wanted him to face the enemy, as he had done on so many bloody battlefields, and their wish was granted.

Time has decimated the ranks of the men who fought through the carnage of the '60s, and only a handful remain in the almost empty Soldiers' Home. But if the home will presently be without a single veteran, owing to the high mortality among them—they are all well up in the eighties—patriotic ladies have rushed into the breach with a view to remedying this deficiency. It is this way:

It appeared, a few years ago, that the widows of the Confederate soldiers, who had been housed in a modest establishment on Grace Street, also were dying off rapidly. The great majority of them were gone, and most of the survivors had a comparatively few years left. Such being the situation, one would have supposed that no further expenditures for quarters for the widows would have been deemed necessary. Certainly, if additional space had been needed, it was available in the rows of empty cottages at the Soldiers' Home.

But at this juncture a truly novel solution was advanced. A magnificent $250,000 Home for Confederate Women was built on the Soldiers' Home grounds! The fact that the widows were fast being gathered to their fathers mattered not at all. In 1932, sixty-seven years after Appomattox, this sumptuous edifice, far more elaborate than anything ever provided for the veterans, was opened with appropriate fanfare. The supply of eligible widows was quite low, but sisters and daughters of veterans were pressed into service. When there are no longer any sisters or daughters, granddaughters will be welcomed into the home. Thus is the Confederate tradition being nurtured in the former capital of Dixie. Whether the Soldiers' Home cottages will be used in the future by sons, grandsons, and great-grandsons of the present inmates is a question which apparently is as yet undecided.

And if Richmonders are zealous in their devotion to the Lost Cause, they are also firm in their allegiance to the Democratic party. It is true that Herbert Hoover carried the city by a small margin in 1928, but everyone now knows why that happened. Not for love of the G.O.P. or passionate devotion to the noble experiment did the capital of Virginia reject the man who bore the standard of the Democracy. But sinister as was the type of prejudice which sent Richmond and Virginia into the Republican column for the first time since the era of Reconstruction, it can at least be said that this prejudice was by no means confined to any state or any section in the political contest in question.

Emphasis likewise should be given to the fact that Richmond's plunge into the camp of the Grand Old Party was in no sense an indication that the Southern Methodist Bishop of Brazil and the Congo enjoys a great personal following in the town. On the contrary, this distinguished counsellor to the erring and the lost once confessed publicly that the wickedness of Richmond depressed him sadly. The city has, in fact, for many years eschewed virtue in its more violent forms.

That is one of the reasons why it is a pleasant place to live. A substantial element of the population stems from the antebellum aristocracy, and whatever else may be said of that aristocracy, it was distinctly libertarian in outlook. The heirs and assigns of these First Families are carrying on in the same tradition today. They believe in a minimum of interference with the habits of the individual, in letting those who desire to do so contract cirrhosis of the liver without benefit of the clergy.

Like their ancestors, again, they recognize the importance of dignified and leisurely living. One finds few traces of the Northern and Western hell-bent-for-election atmosphere on the streets of Richmond. It is one of the country's wealthiest cities of 200,000 population, but few of its inhabitants are engaged in piling up lucre to the complete neglect of more important matters. Prior to the demise of rugged individualism, the place was almost overrun with millionaires, but many of these plutocrats appeared to be interested in other things besides the size of their bank accounts. When the stock market went into its historic tailspin, the wails of anguish were nothing like so loud nor so long as in some other cities.

Citizens of the North and West who form their impressions of inter-racial relationships in the South from the Scottsboro case and other equally disgraceful episodes will find it hard to believe that whites and Negroes live harmoniously side by side in Richmond. But the cordial feeling which prevails is well illustrated by the reception which the city gave the Negro Elks when they had their national convention there in 1925.

The colored Elks had never met in a Southern city before, and they were pleasantly surprised at the reception given them. Segregation ordinances were suspended temporarily. Jim Crow regulations in streetcars and restaurants were forgotten and front porches were made available by many white residents to Negroes who wished to watch the immense parade of 80,000 gaudily uniformed Elks, which took two hours to pass a given point. Most impressive of all was the response made by Henry Lincoln Johnson, Atlanta Negro, to the official welcome extended by Governor E. Lee Trinkle and Mayor J. Fulmer Bright:

"We have been in existence twenty-six years. We met in Boston; the Governor of the state sent a substitute and the Mayor of the city sent his secretary to welcome us. We went to Chicago. The Mayor of that city sent a substitute and the Governor of the state sent his regrets.

"This is the first time in the history of this fraternity that we have heard words of welcome from a chief executive of a state. We assure your excellency that we came to this city with no misgivings at all. We shall go with happy recollections of having been well treated. We are on ancestral ground. . . .

"The men who previously welcomed us had their say, and then they went away. They did not wait to hear what we had to say in reply. We could hear what they said, but they could not hear what we said. But you do. I feel like shouting, 'Governor, oh Governor, safe at home!'"

Richmond, *Gott sei dank*, is in some respects a hick town. Its undertakers are still undertakers, not morticians, and a corpse in their hands is still a corpse, not a "patient." One can walk down the principal business street without a bullet-proof vest in perfect safety. In fact, there hasn't been a first-class murder in the city in years. It has no gangsters, no pineapple throwers; its bootleggers are courteous, efficient, mild-mannered fellows.

And if there is in the former capital of the Confederacy a comparative paucity of young men of felonious intent, there is also a gratifying shortage of robustious backslappers and handshakers. Once in a while this species of fauna clamors that what Richmond needs is a campaign to "boost, talk, and sell" the town to the nation, but such hortatory admonitions usually fall on deaf ears. Even the Chamber of Commerce is manned by persons of intelligence who realize full well that the greatest disaster which could overtake the city would be its conversion into a drab and dismal replica of some of the manufacturing centers in the Middle-Western cow country or the Northeastern beer belt.

It already has been pointed out that much of Richmond's individuality has departed in the wake of the wrecking crew whose axes and sledges laid low a goodly percentage of the mansions remaining as a heritage of the Old South. While some of this destruction could have been prevented, it must be borne in mind that when a city expands steadily into virgin territory, little can be done to preserve the residential property in the older sections, which are no longer fashionable and are occupied in the main by the less fortunate whites and Negroes.

But if Richmond has suffered an "atmospheric" retrogression in recent decades, it has experienced a cultural renaissance. Prior to 1924 it was the only city of more than 100,000 in the United States without a municipal library. In that year a library was opened, and it has grown with remarkable rapidity in usefulness and influence. At about the same time the city had its first week of grand opera, and this became an annual institution until the depression, which played such havoc with all opera, made its continuance impracticable. Even so, at the height of the slump last year a symphony orchestra was launched.

It should not be imagined, however, that the city as a whole prefers Haydn to Irving Berlin, or that the average Richmonder would have any difficulty choosing between, say, a performance of *La Forza del Destino* and a leg show starring Rudy Vallee—for the odds would be overwhelmingly on Rudy and the legs. Similarly, the town is third-rate as a book market. In common with a majority of other Southerners, its inhabitants customarily spend their wampum for almost anything in preference to belles lettres.

One would not be justified, however, in assuming that the denizens of the former chief city of the Confederacy have only a bowing acquaintance with the works of the better writers, for, although they seldom are moved to exchange coin of the realm for those works, they appear to be measurably familiar with their contents. This becomes evident in the conversations one hears in such places as the Westmoreland Club or the Woman's Club. It is true that the dialogues and colloquies at the Westmoreland—which occupies a fine old mansion built by the husband of Poe's "Helen"—have been rather less animated since the bar in the basement was metamorphosed into a cigar counter, but now that the country is returning to sanity in the matter of distilled, malt, and vinous beverages, we may look forward to the raising up at the clubs of another coterie of wits, wags, and raconteurs rivaling their forefathers in verve and sparkle.

During the postbellum years such men as Innes Randolph, poet, sculptor, and musician, and W. Gordon McCabe, teacher, scholar, and historian, were wont to indulge in bits of flashing repartee with any who cared to joust with them over a glass of Burgundy or a mint julep.

Then there was Jo Lane Stern, active in mind and body until

shortly before his death in 1932 at the age of eighty-three, who led the fashionable Richmond German for fifty-one consecutive years. General Stern not only was a prominent figure for more than half a century, but his ready wit was equal to every occasion.

"The ladies—God bless 'em!" was always a favorite toast with these chivalrous sons of the Old Dominion, and there is reason to believe that the belles of that generation, like those of former days, were soothing to the eye.

The celebrated and by no means apocryphal "Virginia hospitality" flourishes in Richmond in a manner as nearly approaching that of before the war as a radically changed mode of life will permit. Contrary to the belief prevalent in some quarters the representative Richmonder is cordial to any outlander who has a decent regard for the amenities irrespective of whether he stems from progenitors of patrician lineage. In fact it is easier to break into Richmond "society" today with a bankroll and no family tree than it is to do so with a tree and no roll—a fact which has resulted in relegating genealogy as a topic of study and conversation to a place in no wise comparable to that which it occupies in such localities as Boston and Charleston.

Richmond in short is aware of its illustrious past without forgetting that it has a present and a future. If the city has been bereft of ancient landmarks which never should have been sacrificed and if its atmosphere is less distinctive than one might expect to find in a place so extraordinarily rich in history, it has achieved a suave compromise, in entering upon its third century, between those of its inhabitants who are afflicted with the get-rich-quick booster complex and those imbued with antebellum and Confederate fixations. The air downtown is heavy at times with the reek of tobacco factories and smoking chimneys, but there is also the emerald sheen of the grass at the Poe Shrine and the arching beauty of the elms as they form a cathedral nave above Franklin Street. Something of the old, something of the new—that is about all one can ask of any city in this era of high-geared salesmanship and raucous ballyhoo.

Monticello

Vegetable garden at Monticello

Charlottesville, from Monticello

Range, University of Virginia

Cemetery near Port Republic battlefield

Stonewall Jackson Statue, Lexington

Narrow-gauge railroad, Blue Ridge Parkway

Looking west from Blue Ridge Parkway

Skyway in the Blue Ridge
(1936)

A mountain highway which is unmatched in the world is being completed in Virginia. It is the Skyline Drive, which will wind along the spine of the Blue Ridge for a distance of from eighty to eighty-five miles at an average height of 3,000 feet above sea level.

Eagles look down from their rocky eyries, and wildcats and rattlesnakes scurry away through the underbrush as the motorist passes along this unique scenic roadway, flanked on one side by the lush Valley of the Shenandoah, which the Indians called the "Daughter of the Stars," and on the other by the rich horse-raising section of Piedmont Virginia.

The entire region is replete with historic associations, extending from the early seventeenth century, when Alexander Spotswood and his Knights of the Golden Horseshoe made their glamorous excursion into the wilderness, down to the Civil War, when the Shenandoah Valley witnessed the hammer blows of Stonewall Jackson and the raids of Phil Sheridan, and the region east of the mountains saw some of the bloodiest fighting of the conflict between the states.

The Corniche Drive, twisting tortuously over the olive-clad and flower-scented Alpes Maritimes from Nice to Menton, and the Amalfi Drive, cut from the cliffs above the blue water of the Gulf of Salerno, are exquisite in their beauty, but in some respects they are inferior to Virginia's mountain boulevard.

And if the Skyline Drive is already unique, it will be even more splendid when present plans for its extension are carried out. The completed portion has its northern terminus at Panorama or

From the *Review of Reviews*, April 1936.

Thornton's Gap, where the Lee Highway between Warrenton and Luray crosses the Blue Ridge. Its southern terminus is at Swift Run Gap, where the Spotswood Trail, linking Gordonsville and Harrisonburg, scales the mountains. An unsurfaced segment thirty miles long extends northward to Front Royal, while contracts have been let for an extension of fifteen to twenty miles on the southern end.

The United States government, which is building the Skyline Drive, already has begun work on an equally stunning mountaintop highway beginning at Jarman Gap, at the lower end of Shenandoah National Park near Waynesboro, and continuing along the crests of the Blue Ridge and Great Smoky Mountains a distance of some 400 miles into North Carolina and Tennessee. This thoroughfare, which will surpass anything of the kind in existence, will terminate in the Great Smoky Mountains National Park.

Most tourists probably will enter the Skyline Drive at the northern terminus, since it is most convenient to the heavily populated northeastern seaboard. Those whose route lies through Washington, only eighty-one miles from the upper end of the drive, will perhaps wish to turn aside and make stops in Alexandria, where the Father of His Country worshipped, and at Mount Vernon, where he lived, as well as to visit the historic fields of First and Second Manassas. Those who find it more convenient to approach the drive directly from the north will pass through Winchester, Washington's headquarters during the Seven Years' War, and the starting point of Sheridan's famous ride to Cedar Creek in the Civil War.

Motorists who prefer to travel in the opposite direction will in all likelihood be desirous of seeing the graves of Lee and Jackson at Lexington, if they are on that side of the mountains, or they will arrange to visit the University of Virginia, with the most beautiful campus in America, the adjoining town of Charlottesville, with the finest equestrian statue in America—Keck's bronze of Stonewall Jackson—and nearby Monticello and Ash Lawn, homes of Jefferson and Monroe, respectively.

But no matter which route to the drive is selected, one may rest assured that it will be over a hard-surfaced highway in good condition and through terrain hallowed by great events. All of northern and eastern Virginia is drenched in history, and a slight deviation from the routes mentioned will take the motorist through battle-torn Fredericksburg, Chancellorsville, and Spotsylvania; to Richmond, former capital of the Confederacy, and on to Jamestown, where America was born; to Williamsburg, Virginia's colonial capital, now in the process of an extraordinarily fine restoration; and to Yorktown, where independence was won. An elaborate system of roadside markers is a great boon to the historically minded visitor.

From whichever end of the Skyline Drive one approaches it, the scenery is arresting.

As the highway climbs higher and higher through the foothills, past old-fashioned Virginia rail fences reminiscent of antebellum days, the air becomes increasingly crystalline and a soft splendor envelops the heights. Sometimes a slight haze, like a velvet mantle, veils the distant peaks. Sometimes a storm breaks over the mountains, thunder rattles among the crags, and all is hidden by rain. Then as the clouds lift, the mountains emerge dimly from the mist, like giants struggling to be free.

In the spring the slopes of the Blue Ridge are covered with the fresh green of budding leaves, interspersed with the flashing white of dogwood blossoms, the deep pink of the redbud, the varicolored trillium, and the trailing arbutus, while violets add their royal purple to nature's palette.

In June the heights blaze with great masses of mountain laurel, the brilliant blossoms contrasting with the glossy leaves of dark green. Summer also brings wild roses, orchids, daisies, and honeysuckle.

Then autumn comes, with all its pageantry, and the mountains and the valleys flame with gold and scarlet. As far as the eye can reach, a carpet of color stretches to the horizon. The wine-red of the maples, dogwoods, and sumacs blends with the yellow and orange of the oaks, maples, and hickories, and with the green of the pines and spruce balsams. Virginia creepers thread the face of gray cliffs with crimson, and trumpet vines wind their bright coils about the dead trunks of oaks that have been shattered by lightning.

The Blue Ridge, it need hardly be said, is not a range of the type of the Rockies or Alps. Its highest peaks, somewhat in excess of 4,000 feet, are wooded, whereas the other ranges mentioned extend far above the timber line, and their jagged and splintered summits are mantled in ice and snow. The beauty of the Blue Ridge is a soft, feminine beauty, whereas that of the Alps, the Andes, or the Rockies, with their glaciers and avalanches, is awe-inspiring and terrible.

It is worth noting, as the National Parks Bulletin has pointed out, that undue importance should not be attached to the elevation of peaks above the sea. Their elevation above the adjacent valleys is often more significant. Hawksbill, for example, towers almost as high above the Shenandoah Valley as the Jungfrau does above Scheidegg, despite the fact that the summit of the Jungfrau is about three times as high above sea-level as the summit of Hawksbill.

Construction of a driveway along the crest of the Blue Ridge presented formidable engineering problems. When one motors over this broad highway today, noting that the grade is nowhere more than six feet in a hundred and that no curve has a radius of less than 200 feet, it is difficult to realize the tremendous obstacles which must have presented themselves when the federal engineers first surveyed this wilderness of crags, canyons, and precipices.

The Blue Ridge happens to be the oldest mountain range in the world. Whether that fact made the going harder or easier, this writer does not know. At any rate, about one-third of the excavation for the thirty-four miles so far completed was through rock.

William M. Austin, highway engineer for the United States Bureau of Public Roads, who ran the original line for the Skyline Drive and was in active charge of construction throughout, deserves much credit for the competent manner in which this amazing job was executed. He functioned under the general supervision of Thomas H. MacDonald, chief of the bureau, and H. K. Bishop, head of the construction division.

On a bright, clear day, one can stand at the northern end of the Skyline Drive and see the Washington Monument, a slender spike stabbing the distant horizon. The motorist who begins his journey at that end soon encounters one of the most extraordinary features of the entire journey—a 600-foot tunnel cut through solid rock. This marvel of highway building is without a counterpart in either hemisphere.

There are no steep grades, no unduly sharp curves, as the highway climbs gradually to the summit of the range. En route one passes hundreds of dead chestnut trees standing like wraiths, their gaunt forms silhouetted against the clouds. They are victims of the blight which has swept over the eastern United States.

At Skyland there is a breath-taking view of the Shenandoah Valley from an altitude of 3,800 feet. Far below, like a ribbon of shimmering silver, the South Fork of the Shenandoah River winds through quiet meadows and past comfortable farmhouses, traversing territory honeycombed by famous underground caverns which are visited by many thousands annually. Beyond, the Massanutten Range rises abruptly. Conspicuous in its face is New Market Gap, used frequently by the armies in the Civil War, and farther on, separated from the Massanuttens by another strip of valley, is North Mountain. Still more distant—across the border in West Virginia—the crest of the Alleghenies melts into the horizon.

Continuing the drive from Skyland, the motorist enjoys striking views, first of the Valley and then of the Piedmont, and occasionally of both simultaneously. At Crescent Rock, where cliffs top 3,000 feet, gnarled and twisted trees bend before the high wind which almost invariably blows. One looks up at towering Hawksbill and down at the valley floor.

The highway continues its winding course to Fisher's Gap, through which Jackson's army rumbled en route to the battle of Fredericksburg. Remains of walls erected at that time to aid the passage of the heavy wagons may be seen. Only a few miles away in the mountains is President Herbert Hoover's former summer camp on the Rapidan.

Occasionally one sees from the drive a wreath of blue smoke

curling up from a sheltered hollow—betraying the presence of the ubiquitous moonshiner. Before the days of the noble experiment the mountaineers in this region made whiskey; they continued to make it, despite federal and state laws, and in the face of battle, murder, and sudden death, after prohibition was enacted, and they are making it today. The Blue Ridge also has been the haunt of desperadoes and feudists. Some of the latter "shot it out" at White Rock Cliffs near the Skyline Drive years ago. Three men lay dead when the last bullet had gone whistling through the trees.

There are crags and canyons along the drive—including exquisite White Oak Canyon, with a stream which drops 2,500 feet in four miles through a gorge of green and white stone—but the road also traverses the big meadows, a flat plateau on the very top of the mountains. This plateau probably will be used by gliders, for the discovery has been made that the currents above the Blue Ridge are particularly conducive to gliding. When Richard C. duPont almost doubled the American gliding record, with a flight of more than 122 miles, he did it with the aid of the currents along this range. Arno B. Cammerer, director of the National Park Service, has announced that an area on the crest of the mountains will be set aside as a national glider camp.

The drive descends gradually as it approaches the southern terminus in Swift Run Gap, where Alexander Spotswood and his Knights of the Golden Horseshoe, a rollicking and bibulous company of swashbucklers, reached the top of the range in 1716 and looked down upon the "Daughter of the Stars." They were almost certainly the first white men who had crossed the Blue Ridge there, and their expedition was an important factor in opening up the western country. A commemorative stone pyramid has been erected in Swift Run Gap by the Colonial Dames.

The Skyline Drive is the most conspicuous attraction of the Shenandoah National Park. Formal dedication of the 200,000-acre tract is scheduled for the late spring. Even before this mountain paradise, ninety miles long and ten miles wide, with its trout streams and bridle paths and camp sites, its birds and trees and flowers, was turned over to the federal government, it attracted more tourists than any national park from coast to coast. When its development is completed, the number of visitors is expected to be vastly increased.

And upon the completion of the projected 400-mile mountain highway into North Carolina and Tennessee, motorists will find it possible to travel in comfort and safety along the backbone of the Blue Ridge and the Great Smokies into the Great Smoky Mountains National Park. Situated on the border between North Carolina and Tennessee, this park is 427,000 acres in extent, and is traversed from end to end by the highest mountain chain east of the Mississippi, with many peaks of more than 6,000 feet. It offers numerous attractions to lovers of the out-of-doors, including the largest variety of plant life found in any equal area on the globe, with 152 separate kinds of trees, and veritable forests of rhododendron, laurel, and flame azalea.

But the Shenandoah Park is situated even more conveniently to the great population centers of the eastern seaboard than its neighbor to the south, and it is more historic. It is one of the garden spots of the earth.

L'Envoi
(1978)

From the time when I joined the *Richmond News Leader* as a cub reporter in 1922 at age twenty-one, I was determined to remain in Virginia. I felt that the old commonwealth was the place for me, the place where my forebears had lived and where I wished to stay. If I may offer a somewhat hackneyed comparison, like Antaeus, the legendary Libyan giant, I have drawn strength and inspiration from the soil of Virginia. Admittedly this is an old-fashioned viewpoint, reminiscent of earlier times when one's native state was exalted to a much greater degree than is customary today. My great-grandfather's love of Virginia caused him to name his new-born son Virginius in 1835. My father's devotion to his father resulted in my inheriting the name. Countless people have asked me how I happened to acquire it.

Being named Virginius involves a few problems, particularly in the area of spelling. The number of ways that Virginius can be misspelled is practically endless. I have a file that includes the following versions, all taken from letters addressed to me:

Virgina, Veretinius, Ziginius, Virgirnia, Virinius, Junius, Berginus, Virgenius, Verges, Virgininus, Vinginius, Virgna, Virginia, Viringuis, Virginios, Virginious, Viginius, Virginiuis, Rivinius, Virgirnis, Vurginius, Wirginius, Virginuis, Virgnus, Virniunius, Virgius, Virginias, Virginiua, Virg, Birgunius, Virgininius, Justinius, Mirginius, Reginos, Miss Virg, Miss Virginiu, Miss Virginia, Mrs. Virginia, and Miss Virginius. There is so much uncertainty as to whether I am male or female that *Who's Who of*

From *Across the Years: Memories of a Virginian* (Garden City, N.Y.: Doubleday and Co., 1978).

American Women forwarded the glad tidings in 1973 that I was being considered for inclusion in that estimable publication.

Furthermore, with a wife named Douglas, the confusion is almost endless. Which led Joseph Bryan III, in a clever rhymed Christmas greeting, to write:

> . . . A mess of collards to the Fred Pollards,
> And cranberry sauce to Bonnie Ross!
> Good health to the Dabneys, Douglas and V!
> (D is the she and V is the he) . . .

Back in 1901 when I was christened, my initials, V. D., were entirely respectable. But in more recent years they have become embarrassing and I no longer use them on handkerchiefs or cuff links. However, they are no more embarrassing than those of Winston Churchill or the late Virginia Congressman S. Otis Bland.

But let us return to my reasons for wishing to spend my life in Virginia. The people are one of the reasons, needless to say. Not all Virginians are charming, of course; in fact some of them are downright boorish and odious. But, on the whole, they strike a high average, and I am happy among them.

I make no defense of the "professional Virginian," that obnoxious and self-centered individual who finds nothing to criticize in the commonwealth, and who spends much of his time knocking the inhabitants of all other states. Over the years, beginning with the article "Poor Old Virginia," which I wrote for the *Baltimore Evening Sun* in 1925, I have sought to point out the Old Dominion's weaknesses and to bring about constructive change.

Another reason that I prefer to live in Virginia is that its politics is probably the cleanest in the United States. The same may be said of Richmond's political climate; in Richmond's city hall graft and thievery are practically unknown. There is rough and tumble "politicating" in Virginia, as elsewhere, for as the late Mayor Richard Daley of Chicago expressed it, "politics ain't beanbag." But the amount of crookedness is at an absolute minimum, and has been for generations.

There are some surprising points of view with respect to the most attractive aspects of life in the Old Dominion. J. St. George Bryan, among the state's greatest wits, once remarked, "Some people think the most enjoyable event that occurs in Virginia is a good old Virginia wedding. But give me a Virginia funeral, with the ladies crying upstairs into silk handkerchiefs and the men drinking good liquor in the basement."

The names of the mountains, towns, counties, rivers, and creeks in Virginia have a flavor all their own. Most of them have English or Indian derivations. Some, like Shenandoah and the Cumberlands, are musical; others, like the Mattaponi River, formed from the junction of the Matta, the Mat, the Po, and the Ni, are quaint. Probably the most extraordinary names are borne by various creeks and rivers, such as Polecat, Toe Ink, Louse, Toots, Whiskey, and Lickinghole creeks, Tin Pot Run, and Stinking River. There is still a post office named Bumpass and another named Negro Foot, but Tightsqueeze changed its name to Fairview some years ago, to the dismay of thousands. It is to be doubted, however, if the Old Dominion can boast of place names as bizarre as Bug Tussle, Oklahoma, or 'T'ain't Much, Alabama.

My decision to remain in Virginia was made early, as previously noted. When I called on my former college-mate Reuben Maury, editorial writer of the *New York Daily News*, in the summer of 1926, I mentioned that I had just had an article accepted by the *American Mercury*. He was obviously surprised, and remarked, "Well, if you've had something accepted by the *Mercury* you certainly don't have to stay in Richmond."

But I *wanted* to stay in Richmond. A newspaper career there appealed to me far more strongly than one in New York, much as I enjoyed being in New York briefly in those days. As a long-term proposition, I had never found the fleshpots of Gotham particularly tempting. Besides, too many young Southerners were being wooed away from their native habitat. This was a major reason why the South had fallen behind the rest of the country.

In 1928 I was interviewed by *Haldeman-Julius Monthly*, a long-since defunct publication. The interviewer wrote, "Virginius Dabney's reason for being in the Old Dominion is a very obvious one. It is that he is a part of it. I doubt that he could write anything that wouldn't betray him to be a Virginian. And when he debunks Virginia, he is more a Virginian than ever."

This may have been intended as a compliment, although it is no secret that a fair number of people from other parts of this country regard Virginians as a supercilious and conceited lot, concerned mainly with their ancestors and looking down their noses at lesser breeds.

About forty years after the above-mentioned interview appeared I was standing at the registration desk of the Palace Hotel in Helsinki, Finland. I had just arrived and had uttered not more than half a dozen words to the clerk when a young man who was standing nearby turned to me and said, "Are you from Virginia?" He was a recent University of Virginia graduate from New York who had recognized my Virginia accent as soon as I opened my mouth.

A reviewer of my history of Richmond wrote in 1977 concerning the author of that opus, "With the possible exception of Robert E. Lee, he probably has a stronger feeling for Virginia than any other man raised south of the Potomac." I never expected to be mentioned in the same breath with General Lee, and the statement seems otherwise to be an exaggeration, but I'll not argue with anybody who accuses me of affection for Virginia.